CW00662139

Inde

Part 1. Bessie's Story 1895-1973

Foreword by Alastair Chambers (Bessie's Son)

Foreword

This epistle-if that's the right name! has been compiled from the scribbling's of Elizabeth (Bessie) Chambers nee Hunter, some even on the back of "junk advertisements" and left on her death to her daughter Nancy Barr

Her son Alastair Chambers after violent protests and a few wee haufs from George Barr the better hauf of the aforementioned Nancy and pleadings and nagging from the female Barr offspring, not to mention the Chambers offspring naggers, finally agreed to Computerise Bessie Chambers' stories.

At the same time it was put into various 'chapters' and the following personal comments made by Alastair Chambers.

A No comment regarding Chapter 1 - this was before my time!

B Chapter 2 - I went to a similar school in the early 1930's, namely Possil Primary in Balmore Road. It had a black ash playground, ideally suited for skinning unwary knees. At Possil School poverty was so bad that one could not go to school with a waterproof or overcoat as it would certainly been pinched out of the cloakroom. This meant that mother had to accompany me to school and return home with outer clothing - four round trips a day for her.

Anyway the school was demolished and rebuilt but the pupils were all sent permanently to Ruchill Primary. Eventually even this new Possil School was closed but it is still there to-day (1987) and is being used to house homeless social security layabouts, teenagers and drug addicts and the like.

Not much of an advance in the intervening 57 years -eh?

D (no c) Regarding Chapter 5, it is certainly true that people visited each other much more often. Most people had not even a radio or a wireless as it was called in those days. We were fortunate to have a wireless which worked fine when Uncle Alex Hunter had not disemboweled the thing. One of my duties was to take the accumulator to the wireless shop for re-charging every week. When Uncle Alex had the wireless working, which wasn't that often, he scared the living daylights out of his young niece Nancy by telling her that the voice came from a man hidden inside.

I don't think that Uncle Willie King and Aunt Mary had a wireless but they enjoyed themselves by singing, their daughter Annie accompanying them on the piano. Annie's boyfriend Andrew was to me at that time a big ten foot tall black haired giant who also could apparently sing. I suppose so could I but naebody would listen.

Anyway my mother, Bessie Chambers, sent me to learn the piano, the teacher being Annie King. We had no piano so I had to practice at my Aunt Mary's house so Aunt Mary knew full well if I missed any practice, but being a good kind Auntie she never told anyone.

However my big cousin Annie could tell by my performance if I hadn't practiced. It has never been decided who was

3

tortured the most - Annie or me. I still cannot play but Annie managed to get me to play a tune called 'Morning Glory' and with two hands too!

E Regarding Chapter 6 - the Arran holiday. Obviously Bessie enjoyed it and the Clarion Camp eventually changed from Corrie to Catacol Bay, to a much larger site well off the road. Any holiday in the hungry thirties was a bonus and the Clarion Camp was cheap. It was very Trade Union and Labour Party orientated and full of left wing cliques - the Turnbulls and the Dicks etc. I did not like it very much (always hungry) and I hated the nightly compulsory singing. I went there 16 years on the trot and have not been back since I was 16 when I got a bike - hurrah - freedom!

F regarding chapters 8 and 9 - my recollections of Aunt Mary and Uncle Willie are (a) digging up his potatoes at Bilsland Drive in the back garden (b) I don't think Uncle Willie could afford to, or did drink, but he seemed to know a lot of songs - one of them a wee bit 'boozie' namely 'Little Brown Jug'. C After the blitz in 1941 he refused to allow Hitler to oust him out of his house at 1672 Dumbarton Road , advising his wife Mary to go to a safer place for a wee while taking his daughters Annie and Bessie with her. He told her 'I'm staying here'. Uncle Willie, Uncle Alex and myself stayed put. Hitler's bombs had got our house so I had no where else to go anyway.

I seemed to get on fine with Uncle Alex. He worked in Babcock and Wilcox at the time in Renfrew. Much to his sister Mary and nieces Annie and Bessie's distress he was interested in making wireless sets so when the living room press door was opened you were immediately attacked

4

without mercy by a sort of living ball of wire about 3 feet spherical diameter and there was no escape . I thought it was really funny and livened up the dark wartime nights, but I kept my big mouth shut, with some difficulty!.

At this time (1941) I was fed at a 'Rest Centre' in Victoria Drive School - you could have anything you liked as long as it was Ambrosia Creamed Rice. I lived for a fortnight on this stuff and have not tasted it since - 46 years!. Now for Bessie's story......

Before we go to Bessie's story let me (Nancy) say a few words about Alastair, my brother. He put together the Foreword brilliantly - a great sense of humour and occasion, all this when he was suffering from Multiple Sclerosis from which he died far too young. I know mum would have applauded his work. Hopefully I can now transfer it on to a modern Laptop as the one Alastair did is fading slightly.......

THIS WAS THE WAY IT WAS - A CENTURY BACK
By
Elizabeth Hall Hunter Chambers

Chapter 1 - Early Years

When I was a few years old I was walking in Argyle Street with my mother. Suddenly there was a furious uproar and we were surrounded by a mob of hysterical people. 'Help me with this infant or she'll be trampled to death' my mother screamed. A powerful man braced his strong muscles, made an opening in the wall of excited people , and lifted me on to his shoulders. From this elevation my fear gave way to perplexity as I gazed on the delirium of this mass of shouting men and women.

Many years later I learned that this was an expression of joy for the relief of a place called Mafeking. I was born a few years earlier on Saint Nicholas day but another mouth to feed could not have been the present my mother welcomed as she lived in constant need.
My birth was the result of an effort to cement a broken marriage but before I was born the fierce quarrels had started again. Father walked out of the home and never returned – it is difficult to apportion blame. My parents were more artistic than practical but the young human demands the latter quality and they could not accept such terms. Because of this we suffered great poverty in the

material sense but happily never spiritually. The poverty that we suffered was never of the spirit.

Mother had three children to support now which she did as adequately as her mercurial temperament would allow by stitching garments called servant wrappers. She often told me that the sewing machine was my lullaby. 'One foot on the cradle and the other on the treadle' she said that four days after I was born she was back at the machine stitching to feed four of us. A kindly neighbour helped mother when I was born. Mrs. Ramsay asked what I was going to call the new baby. My own name is Annie but I do not care for the name. What is your name she *asked? Elizabeth Hall said Mrs. Ramsay. That goes well with her surname so I was given the name of t*he kindly Mrs. Ramsay – Elizabeth Hall Hunter.

Mother's employer was called John McLashan. He was an admirer of Robert Owen and as far as possible applied humanitarian ideals to business methods thus mother received better pay rates for her work than others. She had the reforming urge also but new worlds are not fashioned on the sewing machine. How she hated this thing yet for her bread she was its prisoner. When she was compelled to work at it to get the much needed money her temper was vile and I did not dare speak to her!

When she took me on many visits to the Art Galleries she was a relaxed and lovable parent. Many times I puzzled over her two opposing qualities and sometimes when I got bored at the Art Galleries I felt the same as she must have done when she worked at the sewing machine.

Her lost causes, and those were numerous, made her neglect the job that brought in the money and landed us in constant financial straits. Scarcely any money came from father so she could not afford legal fees to redress the situation. The laws of the country at that time were weighed heavily against the woman who separated from her husband.

Chapter 2- School Days

My sister was ten and my brother was eight years of age when I was born so by the time that I could recognise my environment I was a child in a house of adults. When I was five mother took me to Washington Street School in Anderston along with my favourite chum Annie Mills. After giving particulars as to name, date of birth and so on mother left me.

A hand at the end of a long skinny arm was laid on the top of my head and I was propelled to a seat in a classroom packed with children. The arm repeated the process again and again until all the beginners were gathered. The person then came and stood before us. She was tall gaunt and stern dressed in black from chin to toe. As she walked to and fro her footwear revealed black also. Her hair was black and pulled back fiercely from her face into a bun at the back of her neck. There was not a motherly curve anywhere on her scraggy body .I cowered from her in fear.

We must have looked a dull, listless lot of children as she rounded on us like a drill sergeant with thundering commands like – stand up, sit down, arms up, arms down, arms at front, arms at sides. I watched her in terror fearful that my arms would not do the things she commanded. Suddenly my mother meant everything to me as I howled for her. The skinny arm pointed to the door and she commanded "Get outside till you learn to be quiet".

Glad as I was to be rid of her, my yells booming through the corridors of a strange school were scary too, and I was glad when the skinny arm pulled me back into the classroom. As the school bell rang and we all tumbled out into the playground my fears of the classroom were soon forgotten as Annie Mills and I explored our new surroundings.

In a corner there was a metal container of some kind which had an aperture in the centre. Puzzling over this object we wondered what could be inside. Putting my head inside to find out the darkness scared me and as I jerked my head to get out the jaws of the thing gripped me like a vice.

For the second time that morning I was in disgrace!

After what seemed to be an eternity the skinny arm I had got to know so well negotiated my head to a wide part of the aperture and I was free.

My favourite chums at school were the Seager girls, Jean age 9 and Netta 7 years old. With only 2 children and their father an engineer their living standards were slightly higher than their neighbours.

Mrs Seager was ambitious hoping to escape from where they lived to the Ibrox district, which was a smarter area in those days. The possession of a piano placed a person in the "middle classes" so Mrs Seager hoped for this too as she was sure her daughters were musical. My mother couldn't suffer snobs so Mrs Seager was probably not a snob but she was desperate to escape from her slum environment.

She never mixed with the other neighbours and had friendship only with mother. Maybe the attachment was rooted in the dressmaking mother did for her. Mrs Seager was one of her good customers and her girls were well cared for. Mother attributed this to the family limitation, one of the causes she was advancing at the time.

In our district the hair of most of the girls and many of the boys was verminous which was considered a sign of health. Parents seemed to apply the rats and the sinking ship fable to the head lice and seldom de-loused. Jean and Netta Seager had long chestnut curls dancing down their backs – their heads were scrupulously clean and as I was ordered to play with children who were not verminous Jean and Netta were my constant companions.

In the early years of the century a trade depression hit the country and John Seager lost his job in the wave of unemployment. He had a brother in Sidney, Australia who had offered to sponsor him to come to the new continent and give his family a chance of better living. With all hope of migrating to Ibrox gone they decided to take the offer. His brother sponsored them and soon they had a sailing date. Their room and kitchen house was better furnished than most in the neighbourhood, with strong kitchen table and chairs, wooden fireside chair , oval mahogany table, horse hair chairs, sofa and chest of drawers. The bedding were going to Australia with them. They had depended on the sale of furniture to give them some cash but everyone was poor with the prevailing unemployment – they had no money for furniture, much as they needed it. Our kitchen table was in a sad state , its legs resembled fluted columns with Hector the cat's everlasting sharpening of claws. The depression had not hit our household as servants wrappers were still in demand. This was unusual employment for mother and Mary and Alex was an apprentice so his job was secure. Mrs Seager had hoped to sell her furniture to buy suitable clothing for herself and the girls for the warmer climate they were going to so mother struck a bargain. She would make the clothing in exchange for the kitchen furniture which she needed. I remember the countless yards of nainsook which she made into underwear. Trimmed with fine lace and embroidered with feather stitching Mrs Seager was delighted and promised mother the square of wax cloth off the floor as an extra. When the furniture arrived, our kitchen, though always untidy looked more comfortable except to Hector whose ears were constantly boxed if he went near the table.

We took farewell to our friends who were quite happy to leave the poverty of their native land and journey to a new life so very far away.

It was a long, long time before a letter came back from Mr Seager from Sidney saying that Mary his wife had taken ill as the boat sailed through the Suez Canal. A few days later she died of appendicitis and was buried at sea

I had been many weeks at school when Annie Mills my chum fell ill with measles. Most mothers in the tenement coped with this illness without the help of a doctor but in Annie's case complications developed and the Parish doctor diagnosed pneumonia when he called.

Mother was seldom demonstrative to us but somehow we learned that we meant a great deal to her nevertheless. It surprised me that one day during Annie's illness she held me close to her saying "Annie has fallen asleep and will never go to school with you again".

Mother believed that all happenings in this life should be faced courageously so at five years of age I was taken to see my little dead chum. The cotton sash curtain was drawn across the window in the one apartment house, the fire was unlit and a white table cover was draped over the dresser where the remains of Annie lay in her little white coffin. Mother lifted me up to see Annie and held me very close as if to cushion any shock I may feel. She need not have worried, as Annie's mother bared her face I was filled with admiration and envy.

Annie's lovely face, her beautiful long brown hair, face like wax, the satin lined coffin adorned with silver (I was sure that it was silver). Those gorgeous white cords! They would make lovely skipping ropes.

Annie's mother invited me to "touch her wee brow and you will not dream about her" I did not dream about Annie but the sensation of a wee hot palm on a cold, cold brow never left me.

The two mothers were talking in whispers and drying their eyes on the hem of their white aprons.

"When can I get a beautiful box like that to lie in?" came a little voice from the silence.

The two mothers were totally shocked!

Chapter 3 – Moving House

Within the next two years circumstances in the home made it imperative for us to move to the South Side of the city. My sister Mary was working as an assistant in the warehouse where mother was employed and my brother Alex was an engineering apprentice with the Fairfield Shipbuilding Company working from 6a.m. until 6p.m. This meant rising at 4.30a.m. to kindle the fire in order to have a meal also two lots of 'pieces' for meals during the working day. To make things easier the removal was arranged.

As we were coming down three flights of stairs and up four it seemed intensely exciting.

The coalman's lorry was booked to transport our few possessions. "See and bring a sturdy looking beast" mother commanded and clean up your lorry – I do not want coal dust all over my beds!

The brawny animal was important as mother was devoted to all dumb creatures.

How I hated being in the street with her when she would meet a horse with it's rib cage showing or knobbly knock knees or if it looked tired. If the carter used the whip on the horse she would face up to him shaking and shouting threatening with the law while shaking her fists.

What a flood of filthy invective poured over her on those occasions and I tried to restrain her pleading with her not to say anything to the carter if his horse looked too thin. I will not ignore cruelty to a dumb animal what kind of coward are you?

The horse met with mother's approval on the night of the removal and the 'flitting' was on its way across the Jamaica Bridge. Mother, Mary and I crossed by ferryboat carrying our best clothes and mother's warehouse work. It was very dark with feeble gas jets on the dockside casting puny shafts of light. As the little vessel slipped from the steps it gave a warning 'TOOT' which so alarmed Hector our black cat who was wrapped in a shawl that it took the three of us to hold him down and prevent him disappearing into the river.

The house that we had moved to lay at the top of four flights of dark stairs – a kind of Baronial staircase with two houses on each landing and two in a wooden lobby. Even in midsummer we went up and down in half light and as with sightless people our auditory senses became highly developed. Seventeen families lived in the close with no hot water tap anywhere. Evil smelling industries surrounded us, Engineering Works, Chemical Works, Paint Works and the local Gas Works not forgetting the Tar Factory. In such conditions the efforts of women to keep house and families reasonably clean was very disheartening.

Family planning was at this time almost unknown so there were other compensations. We shared a back court with three similar closes so it was easy to assemble fifty children for singing games, wee shops, houses and schools. In this way lack of boredom counteracted lack of beautiful surroundings.

I was eight years old when we moved to West Street in the South Side of Glasgow. My playmates were very friendly, enquiring about my parents, sister and brother – even Hector the cat.

The question of my father worried me and I wished him to fit into conventional patterns. How could I tell my wee friends that he lived in Edinburgh and I had never seen him? This was my opportunity and I seized it with relish. "You have no father"? They asked. "No" I replied. "Is he dead"? They asked. "Yes" I continued. "Was it a long time ago"? They persisted. Bringing a sob to my voice I replied "Just about a year ago". It was Double Pneumonia. Then where is he buried? This question almost failed me because I did not know the names of any cemetery in Glasgow so I told them he was buried in a churchyard in the Highlands.

Morag Chambers has done some good work in tracing my grandfather (Bessie's father) and recently she found out that he lived in the Craiglockart area of Edinburgh, I think his name was James Hunter. He died at the age of 52 from Tuberculosis which was prevalent at that time. He died in the poorhouse which was really as low as you could go so not a blissful ending and may have been better staying with his wife a children in Glasgow. I believe he had a son also called James. It was also recorded that he was the widower of Annie Howieson (Hunter) which was untrue as she died when she was 84 so something funny here. He may have committed bigamy with the lady he took off with when he left his wife and children but who knows? Back now to Bessie's Story..............

I had never known grandparents and longed for a granny in a cottage beside a glen in the Highlands so this was another longing fulfilled. I often asked mother "are you sure I don't have a granny in the highlands"? I was assured that I certainly did not have any granny in the highlands and that my mother's forefathers belonged to Glasgow since Glasgow was anything! I replied that I would like to have been highland. "Why be a belly crawler to a Duke in the highlands"? My reply was that nobody really wants to say that they belong to Glasgow. "Your forefathers all survived the plagues and I will always be proud to say that I belong to Glasgow.

Having got rid of my father I created someone I had always longed for – and wound a fairy tale round a wee sister aged three

I told my friends that we were very rich when father was alive and had to leave our big house to come here. I described my father's funeral, the hearse then the open carriage filled with flowers and the sixty men who attended it.

When they asked where my wee sister was I told them a rich Aunt who has a farm in the Highlands took Elspeth to live with her as she had no family of her own and thought that my mother had plenty of children to look after.

Shortly after the episode s of my made up stories mother met a neighbour on the stair of the close and she asked her if she was a widow. "I've been a widow for the past seven years" she replied pulling the same sad face that I had worn at the first 'murder'.

The kitchen was square in our new two apartment house, cooking being done in an open fireplace, which together with the window filled one wall. On the wall running at right angles to this was the coal bunker, Dresser with pot cupboard beneath and two shelves above. The bed which was set in to the wall and the meat cupboard faced the fireplace. The kitchen table and chairs stood at the remaining wall. They were made of whitewood and had to be scrubbed regularly.

The sewing machine with its chattering rhythm dominated our lives and occupied the best place in the kitchen – during daylight hours at the window and at the fire when darkness came. Underneath the gas bracket stretched a slim brass arm with an incandescent light on it where mother did her sewing.

Our fireplace was a source of shame to me as in the homes of our neighbours it was burnished with emery cloth and black lead which made it a flashing living thing giving warmth and a sense of plenty in the midst of such drabness. Mother painted ours with black stove enamel which to the housewife of the period was desecration.

I described the gleaming beauty of the fireside next door, venturing to win her over to more conventional ways.

"I quite believe that Mrs. Stewart's fireplace is dazzling" she retorted but it would fit her better if she would polish up her mind a bit – she's almost a halfwit! The senseless scouring of a house is not in my programme. Any spare time I may have is spent enjoying the real things of life such as reading, Art Galleries and Museums.

To this end she was dedicated, the kitchen was constantly untidy and half-finished garments littered the Dresser, bed and chairs while cloth clippings littered the floor.

Chapter 4 - The New House

The room which my brother Alex had matched this mess as he had an inventor's impulse. Plans for central heating were drawn up for our two apartment slum by Alex. He brought pieces of metal from the shipyard to make a model and an engineer's vice was fixed to the room table. As cloth clippings made their little mounds in the kitchen, iron filings did likewise in the room. Except for a square of material called 'waxcloth' there were no other floor coverings to worry about.

In Alex's room there was a bed, chest of drawers, a few chairs and mother's 'alter piece' – the book case. A tiny bust of John Knox sat on top of the book case but I never learned what affinity my agnostic mother had with him – unless it was the price of 3d at the 'barrows'.

Mother's taste of literature was of the best and she had a library of novels, poetry, essays and travel.

The untidiness of our home was not wholly bad as it bestowed a Bohemian freedom, nourished the imagination, and developed individualism by its very unconformity. I had endless amusement to no one's annoyance. Mother kept us constantly on the stretch always reaching higher than we could go.

When I was nine years old Andrew Lang was my favourite author. He wrote books such as 'The Green Fairy', 'The Yellow Fairy', and 'The Pink Fairy' and so on. The stories all began 'Once Upon A Time' and they all ended 'And They Lived Happily Ever After'. Such a cosy tidy world that was soon to be shattered for me. When are you going to grow up?

Mother exclaimed. "Time that you're reading was a bit more advanced!"

A library was collected and bought foe a few coppers at the 'barrows'. 'Lambs Tales from Shakespeare' the 'Water Babies', 'Silas Mariner', 'Arabian Nights Entertainment', 'Rab and His Friends', 'Poe's Tales of Mystery and Imagination' and 'The Tanglewood Tales'. I did not like her choice but somehow children sense that parents know better.

I liked when mother was finishing the wrappers with a row of buttonholes on each bodice. As she stitched with firm regular stitches I sat on the floor at her feet threading needles for her and making tiny dolls from the clippings lying around.

She had a pleasant voice and a repertoire of Scots Ballads, one in particular was 'Jessie's Dream' which I found quite heartrending. I pictured Jessie surrounded by black Indian faces at Lucknow, dreaming of Bonnie Scotland and her home in the Highlands.

Mother's voice was pleasant but my sister Mary's voice was one of exquisite beauty. Being the time of Gilbert and Sullivan she got a copy of The Mikado from the library. In the jumble of cloth rags, iron filings and peevor beds Mary battled with 'The Moon and I'. My singing voice did not measure up to this standard but mother being careful that I was not left out got me books of poems and I was made to memorise them. I felt rewarded when I won a Silver Medal at an I.O.G.T. musical festival in the Waterloo Rooms. The title of the poem was "THE DYING CHILD'S APPEAL TO HER DRUNKEN FATHER".

Mother had strange ideas about health saying that only degenerates were ever ill – we were never ill.

The fever van was horse drawn in those days and carried a little tinkling bell on its harness. When we heard this we swarmed after it to see the little patient wrapped in blankets being carried off to Ruchill Hospital which was the infectious diseases hospital.

I was spotted from the window on one such occasion and ordered upstairs. As soon as I reached the door she bellowed "What were you doing at that van when I have told you not to go near them"? Before I could think of a good reason she yelled on "What's going to happen to my warehouse work if you bring infectious diseases into the house"? I was stuck for words and no sound came through the tension of fear I felt for having endangered the warehouse work. The Sanitary fumigated houses that had infectious diseases and this would not have bode well for the warehouse work. My defences suddenly came to my aid and I timidly suggested that I would not get fever if she would buy me a camphor locket, every girl wears them I said and they only cost a penny. "There are certainly no pennies here for superstition and witch-doctoring" she scoffed.

Chapter 5 - Before Television

A circle of good friends often visited us and no extra preparations were made for them so they just dropped into the entanglement. Miss Dick was one of the friends who looked after her father and her task was not made easy as he had a strong Calvinist fibre in him. Comfort, to his way of thinking was godlessness so their room and kitchen house looked like two empty barns with a few articles of furniture and no furnishings – so unlike our disorder! Nevertheless Miss Dick loved to visit us as she was drawn to Spiritualism and mother's agnostic leanings by way of theosophy were also turning that way. They discussed spiritual guides and manifestations to their mutual pleasure.

Miss Dick suffered from some sort of muscular rheumatism and mother would give her muscles a gentle massage. She insisted that mother had 'healing hands' but this ten year old sceptic wandered what was so different from 'healing hands' and a camphor locket!

Another friend arrived on holiday from America bringing gifts of perfumed soap and toilet water – the scent was just grand and I thought that America must be a lovely sweet smelling place. Her husband left Glasgow during one of the trade depressions and they now lived in an ugly town, expanding rapidly with the motor car industry.

Mrs. McInnis made the journey home from America with her three children who had been left with her mother when she made the visit to us.

She was in great distress as she unfolded her problems to mother saying that she did not want to go back to America and was seeking advice. Mother's advice was to go back to Fred as he was a hard working fellow who had been able to pay their fares home and she had lots of luxuries mother never had. Mrs. McInnis still insisted that she was tired of him as he was so dull saying that money was not everything. Mother replied that it was the want of money that was her worry and being chained to the sewing machine which she hated like hell. "I thought that you would have advised me – you've got along without a man" she observed.

"Listen Jessie "snapped mother "the whole world is against you when you separate from a man, and you get no sympathy"

Mrs. McInnis was taken aback by the sharpness of mother's tongue and tearfully she told of her longing for Scotland and her hatred of America. She took mother's advice however as some weeks later we took farewell of her leaving the Clyde, the land she loved to return to the man she did not love.

At times our relations called and mother was an enigma to her sisters-in-law. They were bores to her so visits were infrequent. Their literary tastes were poor and never got beyond. "Peoples Friend" or "Weekly Welcome" which in mother's estimation was as low as you could get.

Her "Guid Sisters" were shocked when she appeared in blouses made by herself which were very stylish and also her hair dressed into little rolls framing her face in a youthful way. They told her that she looked thirty years of age instead of forty.

An uncle called one evening to tell us that his wife had given birth to a baby girl. Mother told him that it was disgusting bringing another child into a single end house when there were already five other children but he saw nothing disgusting about having another child. After a cold silence she asked him what the baby's name was. "We thought we would call her Annie after you" said Uncle Alex.

Chapter 6 – Holiday Time

I was ten years old when I spent my first holiday away from home but there was nothing unusual in this pattern.
Holidays were not financially possible for most people in our area. The ailing ones sometimes had a few weeks rest in the convalescent homes organised by benevolent societies but mother despised those institutions.
Our family kept in very good health mostly due to her progressive ideas on diet. Ours contained mainly fruit and vegetables as far as money would allow and she almost dared us to be ill.
Mother was an enthusiastic member of the Clarion movement which was a fellowship not purely political organising many excellent activities such as Choirs, Drama Groups, Cycling Clubs and a field club for rambling and the study of fossils, wild life and flowers. There was also a Camping Club which took place in Arran during the Fair Holiday period.
My first holiday at the Clarion Camping Club was with my elder sister Mary and her boyfriend. The camp was based at Corrie and I boasted plenty about it to my chums as this was quite an adventure for me, but they were quite uninterested. Had I been going to Saltcoats, Dunoon, Gourock or Rothesay that may have excited their envy but as they had never heard of Arran they simply looked at me in bewilderment. This island to them was more remote than the moon to the modern child. In those days no one except tinkers and soldiers slept under canvas.

The simple life in second hand army bell tents could be most complicated in wet weather. Among the hills of Arran it is often rainy and the rain trickled through the walls of the tent making pools in the tarpaulin groundsheet.

The clothing of the period was heavyweight and we wore layers of clothes taking hours of sunshine to dry them. Blankets, bed linen and towels and a change of clothing and footwear had to be packed the clumsy articles taking up much space. Blankets were 'doublers' only and were not made in 'singles'. Skirts were ankle length, three and a half yards wide. Mary's blouses were of a voile material with a yoke lace insertion, the collar was to the throat and sleeves to the wrists. I had a navy long sleeved dress, worn to the calves, one print dress and several pinafores. There were no waterproofs or Macintoshes as they were then called. The weather was fairly kind to us so they were not missed. Our belongings were packed in a tin 'kist' and a container called a Japanese Hamper, a kind of box made from a yellow grass like substance, having no locks and bound together with leather straps.

On 'Fair Saturday' morning, along with fifty or more fellow campers, we left the Glasgow Central Station for Arran. There were no over forties in this company and most of them were under twenty years of age. The train journey to Wemyss Bay was sheer joy with a compartment full of over excited youths, all of the choristers and everyone singing. Being the heyday of Gilbert and Sullivan Operas they were sung with gusto. They learned the musical score from their seats in the 'gods' in the theatre and even my immature mind was captivated by the tuneful compositions.

The train rushed on past Langbank to meet the steamer where a cleaner River Clyde widened into a lovely estuary – a view of the river from a hillside which I had never seen before and can remember with pleasure.

At Wemyss Bay I was spellbound being covered with glass like a Botanical Garden – hanging baskets filled with flowers, tubs with greenery in them, everything spotlessly clean, the tang of the salty sea everywhere. The steamer King Edward was already at the pier waiting for us. My brother Alex told us the previous night that she and her sister ship Queen Alexandra were the new turbine driven ships and had no paddles. I missed the exciting churning paddles and the foamy soapy water they made at the piers.

There was no pier at Corrie so a ferry boat awaited the steamer. On deck a portion of the gunwale was opened and a rope ladder went over the side of the ship. It was no easy exercise for the women negotiating this wobbly stairway – with skirts to their ankles, picture hats held on the head with hatpins like skewers, plus the motoring scarves used for wearing on board ship. Our ankles had to be modestly covered at all times which was very hard with the swaying of the ship and bobbing of the ferryboat. When my turn came I was tossed into the arms of an oarsman and placed on a seat of a rowing boat. For the first time of my life it did not seem real.

After fifty campers with luggage had been ferried to the jetty, we set off for the camp site one and a half miles away. Though laden with coats and a net bag full of extra footwear, Mary struggling with the Japanese Hamper and Willie her boyfriend with the tin 'kist' I was captivated by the beauty of this lovely island. Every stone, pebble and shell on the beach was so clean and white and Bell Heather, Bog Myrtle, Wild Iris and Forget-me-not sprouted from the fissures on the rock face. Mother, brother and home in the slums were completely erased from my mind as I embraced this life close to nature.

The road that ran around this island cut through our camp which was situated by a clear gurgling stream. The row of bell tents were on the foreshore and across the road on a patch of level ground, close to the hillside, a heavy tarpaulin was nailed to a square framework to make what was called the galley tent where the cooking was done.

Close to the galley tent a trench fire was dug in the ground where porridge and soup were cooked in huge iron pots. The fire was never allowed to go out and in the evenings the campers gathered around for concerts.

The meals were simple consisting of porridge, bacon, boiled eggs for breakfast, soup, boiled mutton or sausages and semolina and prunes (usually singed) for dinner. At tea time we had cheese or boiled ham. There were no tinned foods of any kind in those days. In good days we sat on the grass and ate our meals but if it was wet they were served in the tents.

Six adults and two children occupied our tent and the floor was covered with a stout groundsheet on top of which we laid a heavy bedmat. Rolled in our blankets we were quite snug at nights and the leaves of the bracken were stripped to stuff our pillowcases and the addition of bog myrtle made them fragrant.

During the week a party from the camp arranged to climb Goat Fell to see the sunrise from the peak. They left in the evening, the men in tweed jackets, Norfolk style, Donegal hats, Knickerbockers and top hose with stout boots. Slung on each shoulder was an oblong tin box called a vaseulum packed with sandwiches for a meal during the climb. When empty they held specimens of plant life, stones and fossils. The girls wore white linen skirts to their ankles and black woolen stockings and heavy shoes or boots along with long sleeved blouses with thin motoring scarves on their heads. In those outlandish clothes they conquered Goatfell but the white linen skirts lay in the burn for a day to remove the bog that stained them to the knees.

There were six children in the camp and one of our favourite amusements was playing "wee shops". How well stocked they were from things that lay to hand – sand for sugar, oatmeal and flour. Iris leaves for leeks and other plants for parsley, pebbles for potatoes and small eggs for sweets – shells, wilks and seaweed – we played endlessly day after day in the sweet air as yet not fouled by the motor car. There were some interests back home that I missed, one of them being the newspapers. At least one part of the newspaper, the column entitled "Accidents and Fatalities" which appeared in the Evening Citizen, each paragraph giving a detailed account of those happenings in the City. It could be that someone had overbalanced and fallen into the well of the close or out of a window into the back court or even a child crushed to death under a bread van. There was the woman who fell under a tramcar which had to be jacked up!

If the column in the Evening Citizen occupied the length of the page I was thrilled but if it was only half a column I felt that the human race had let me down. If however a horse fell down in the street or a cat got under a tramcar I wept hysterically. I may have missed the Evening Citizen but I was to view something in Arran that put the casualty column into eclipse!

One day the campers had a picnic to Glen Sannox and at the small graveyard we stood around the grave of a man called Rose who was murdered on Goatfell. Evidently he had been lured up there and pushed over a precipice. There was a large boulder on the grave and we were told that the body had been hidden underneath.

This was far better than anything displayed in the "Police Budget" in the newsagent's window back home.

Our camp was always very tidy as it had grown out of the Field Club where three rules were strictly observed: "To open the bye ways", "To steek the yetts", "To leave our halting places free from litter".

There was great interest in plant life and as children we were instructed in the names of wild flowers and trees and told never to willfully destroy them because we had enjoyed their beauty and had a duty to pass the pleasure on to those who come after us

A choir was formed at the camp which rehearsed all week and gave a concert on the jetty singing "Since First I Saw Your Face", "Drink to me Only", "Sweet and Low", "When other Lips" and "The Lass O' Arranteenie".

A quartet sang "Brightly Dawns our Wedding Day", Mary sang "The Moon and I" and a tenor sang "A Wandering Minstrel".

There was also a comic singer but I do not remember the song or patter and the concert ended with "The Comrades Song of Hope". There was a good appreciative audience of both natives and holidaymakers.

The time came for striking camp and going home but during the holiday I had collected empty toffee tins filling them with shells and pebbles for taking back home. Mary was struggling to pack the 'kist'and hamper with un-ironed clothing that was bulkier than ever! When I presented her with the boxes of shore treasure she promptly rejected them which led to a battle. There was compromise in the end and she packed the tins.

I was in the first ferry load to board from the side of the ship when the ferry arrived with a bunch of wild flowers and bell heather in one hand and my 'pieces' in the other. I gazed out on this fairyland island and as the boat drew away felt a deep sadness such as I had never experienced before.

Chapter 7   Back home to reality

When we moved to the South Side mother gave some consideration to the school I was joining. She had a choice of three, Centre Street School being the nearest, but it looked squalid and to use her own phrase "I would not put my cat in it" thus putting Centre Street School out.

The choice now lay with Scotland Street School and Crookston School. Mother liked the look of Scotland Street School but Mary thought that it was too far away and mother agreed although she would have liked me to have gone there as it was such an unusual building which appealed to her. I had to be home at four o'clock sharp to take mother's work to the warehouse twice a week.

I was therefore enrolled at Crookston Street School which was built in 1884 – a collection of grey sandstone buildings enclosing four small playgrounds, two for girls and two for the boys, surrounded on three sides by tall tenements and on the remaining side by blocks of warehouses and offices. High up on a wall in the girl's playground was the school bell which the janitor tolled. He was a delightful person with dark brown hair, eyes that always seemed to be smiling and a neat beard which gave him a sort of seafaring look. He was usually a few minutes early for bell ringing and would join the row of girls for skipping ropes, his bearded face bobbing up and down making us giggle helplessly. When playing peevor beds he would pretend to kilt up his skirts as we did when jumping from box to box. When he released the rope for tolling the bell he had to struggle with amazon like girls trying to pull him away.

Before the bell was silent, we stood in orderly rows facing a stern male teacher who shouted commands to us in military fashion. For us discipline started before we entered the school building.

Miss Brown my teacher was a pleasant looking person with dark hair which she wore in a sausage shaped roll framing her face the back hair being in a bun at the nape of her neck. She had a very full black skirt reaching almost to the floor and brush braid on the hem. She wore a black shirt blouse held neatly in place with a tightly drawn belt at the waist. The black of the neckline was brightened by a piece of white lace or Swiss trimming.

Our classroom was almost square and on one side was the glass partition separating us from the class next door and facing this were two large double windows. One blank wall was facing us and on this wall was the Attendance Board with its chalk mark of 53 children most days and also a map of the world. This was the only bit of colour in the room which was painted a drab brown. The teacher's desk, a wastepaper box and a blackboard completed the furnishings.

If we had not known that we were "children in the 20th Century" our books would have told us. There was the "Twentieth Century Reader", the "Twentieth Century Jotter" and "Twentieth Century Notebooks". Miss Brown's enthusiasm for the "Twentieth Century" prodded our imagination, keeping it at full stretch to grasp the importance of the period in which we lived.

It was a wonderful time – Marconi having recently thrown wireless waves across a vast ocean. There was also the discovery of X rays, penetrating the strongholds of skin, muscle and tissue to the bones beneath. Gorgeous palaces were rising everywhere, baubles on a ribbon of celluloid, spooling the entire earth. I always loved Geography and owe the fondness of this to Miss Brown who made the subject so colourful. She would tell us that every country coloured red is yours and it made us feel just great!

She would emphasize that we were natives of Scotland and Scotland is part of Great Britain and all those countries coloured red were part of the British Empire, upon which the sun never sets. She then

explained why the sun never sets on the Great British Empire.

She tried to explain the vastness and power of the Atlantic Ocean by taking us on an imaginary cruise from the Clyde to America telling us that our steamboat may have to struggle with waves as tall as the buildings opposite and for four days we would not see land at all.

As we had only crossed the Clyde on a ferry and had just seen ripples on the river we found her description of the Atlantic unbelievable. Unfortunately the great ocean was having it's power diminished. On another continent a frail craft had risen a few feet in the air, so with this conquest the children that Miss Brown was teaching would be able to cross her mighty, magnificent Atlantic in the space of a few hours – for this was the great 20th century!

We did not have bombs to scare us in those far off days but we had to cope with serious illnesses such as Scarlet Fever, Diphtheria and Rheumatic Fever which would absent a child from school for three to six months.

Girls would come back, shorn of their hair and looking like little collaborators of a time yet to come and feeling just as ashamed . They occupied the front seats so that Miss Brown could give them extra tuition to bring them up to class standard. Sometimes she used the brighter pupils to assist her in this work as working together was good fun and excellent character training.

When we did not have backward scholars to help she filled the front seats with the bad hand writers. On several occasions I was included in this group.

For our lesson we wrote the word 'minimum' dozens of times. Upstroke of the pen was light and down stroke was heavy and all legs of the letters had to be neat and of the same length.

We then went on to maxims such as – 'Early to Bed, early to Rise' etc., 'Honesty is the Best Policy' and 'Neither a Borrower nor a Lender Be'.

The 1906 earthquake in San Francisco took place when we were in Miss Brown's class. As the grim news leaked through she explained the awful happenings when such a disaster involved a town. Great chasms swallowing up the buildings - the terrible death toll.

There was another upheaval of a political kind in Britain – the 1906 General Election with its victory for the Liberal Party. Miss Brown must have been a Liberal when she told us so much about it.

I can recall several worries that we children had about this time – maybe it was adult talk we heard. On rainy weather sitting on the tenement stairs, we discussed in our childish way, the German menace. We thought that the Germans had designs on our British Empire.

Another worry was the yellow peril which we heard and believed that horrid little Chinese and Japanese people would overrun the white people.

Then one awful Monday night we discussed and waited for the end of the world due the next day!

Chapter 8   Sister Mary and William King

We now had regular visits from one of Mary's admirers. His name was Willie King.

Mary was in her early twenties and Willie was in his late thirties and as there was a seventeen year age gap mother was almost intractable about a marriage with such a difference in their ages.

As she got to know him better however and learned his reasons for late marriage, she did not hesitate to give her approval.

Willie was the eldest of three boys and at seven years of age lost his mother to Tuberculosis, his father dying of the same illness when he was twelve years of age.

After his father died an Aunt looked after them until the relatives conferred to decide what could be done for them. Willie remembers part of the discussions which clouded the future of the three little boys. Everyone was scared of the word 'Consumption' in case they were 'smitten'. Most of the relatives made various excuses not to take them in to their homes and suggestions were made to send them to Quarrier's Homes where they would be well looked after and probably sent to Canada later on where they would get a good chance in a new country. Willie remembered this discussion all his life.

The aunt they were living with was horrified at the thought of her sister's children being sent to an orphanage so although she had seven children of her own she agreed to give them a home with her. They lived in a room and kitchen house and her husband's earnings as a labourer were eighteen shillings per week (90 pence). The 'Parish' gave them a few shillings towards the keep of the boys.

Willie's childhood memories were of four children sharing a bed and going barefoot for seven months of the year, of holes in the seat of his trousers through which the tail of his shirt poked out and of constant hunger pangs.

The first of these did not worry him much as bed mates were cosy in the winter and he slept like a puppy anyway. The second memory was a painful one as the cruel touch of cold pavements in early spring and late autumn and the numerous cuts with broken glass and rusty nails which caused wounds to become infected.

He overcame and suffered the hunger pangs but the injury that the ragged seat of his trousers inflicted on his self-respect was a memory he could not erase.

Auntie Mary worked hard but food, clothing and shelter for ten children and two adults on little more than a pound a week was an impossible task. Willie said that he often hungered for food but never for affection – had she given plenty of that to the entire little brood.

There were no three course dinners for them as they lived on carbohydrates - the filling foods. Sometimes for a special treat the huge frying pan would be piled high with oatmeal and onions with beef dripping and sizzled on the hob filling the kitchen with appetizing smells.

The family lived in the Dennistoun district of Glasgow and at week-ends and school holidays Willie and his chums walked barefoot into a new world which was Hogganfield Loch.

Here they learned to swim and to enjoy the sun on little naked bodies and to feel the moist caressing touch of grass on bare feet. Willie was passionately fond of nature study and this spot with its flowers, grasses, birds and berries, trees and butterflies was paradise for him.

He set out to find the names of birds, trees and wild flowers and being a patient person he acquired a substantial knowledge of the countryside.

To help with the feeding problem at home the three boys were educated at the Rottenrow Day Industrial School where at mid-day they got a bowl of soup and bread.

When Willie was thirteen years of age he was Dux of the school and received a book prize which was a thin book containing the Lord's Prayer. The following year he was top boy again and was given another religious book entitled 'One Hour a Week' a bible lesson for the young.

He had hoped for books on the new sciences and inventions that were spurring the Industrial Revolution in the last quarter of the 19th Century. His disappointment was intense and in adult life did not have the desired allegiance his school directors had intended. At eighteen years of age he became an agnostic and died sixty years later without faith.

Of Auntie Mary's family of seven, four died quite young of tuberculosis and three emigrated. In her old age she was comfortable and cared for by her sister's three boys who had shared her humble home.

Chapter 9 Brother Alex

A few years before the 1914-18 war Alex completed his final
year of his apprenticeship in Pembroke Dock in Wales. He
was one of a party of tradesmen sent from Fairfield Shipyard,
Govan to fit out the H.M.S. Bellona with her engines.
Mother was quite pleased and adjusted to the idea. Alex
and become a bit moody and unsettled - an individualist
living a life apart from us in books.
Alex hated slums and poverty but they were his bedmates
for the first twenty years of his life. As he matured he went
deeper and deeper into literature and art , withdrawing
from the family.
The year spent at Pembroke Dock did him good as he was
fortunate in his lodgings having a room to himself in a five
apartment terrace house. When he had been there some
time a letter with a black border around the envelope came
from his landlady.
We all feared the mourning notepaper but the letter it
contained was full of information and warmth. She had
recently lost a son; a studious boy with his head
continuously in books and Alex would be a heaven sent
blessing to her as he was the same type of person. The year
that he would be staying with her would help her over a
harrowing experience. His landlady was a very kind person
and sent them crab apples and boat shaped Christmas pies.
When H.M.S.Bellona was fitted out Alex went on her trial
trips which he and the crew found very much of an ordeal
due to the excessive rolling which made them violently sea
sick.

He was happy to see the last of H.M.S.Bellona and left Wales for home but he was fated to see her again from the deck of a Destroyer in World War 1. As they passed each other he reflected on the horrors of seasickness he had endured.

Alex was home only a few months when sister Mary and Willie King decided to marry and as was normal at that time the Reception was held in the house.

I'll never know where mother stored her warehouse stuff but for the first time in my twelve hears the house was tidy! It had to be tidy as the house was packed with guests.

Mother helped by Mary did her own catering which was excellent considering that it had to be cooked over an open fire. At times such as those culinary skills were exceptional but at other times quite dreadful as we never knew what would appear on the plate but we ate it all as such was mother's temper that we did not dare to complain!

I have a theory that her preference for a vegetable diet and fruit was an effort to escape cooking. Mother could never have been a hostess in the acceptable sense of ruling over a table.

Nevertheless she had many visitors and friends who came to see her, sometimes in great distress but would unburden themselves once a pot of tea appeared.

The wedding receptions were really good and all the relations were there including children which do not always happen in to-day's world. Everyone was relaxed and guests with good voices would entertain with the audience joining in.

The songs as I remember them were loaded with sentiment such as 'Genevieve', 'Kind, Kind and Gentle is She' and

'We'd Better Bide a' Wee'. There then came the songs of the emigrants baring their hearts for Scotland in some foreign land. Aunties and Uncles took you on their knees telling you how you had grown and how bonnie you were. Everyone was happy and most of them gave us a song.

There was no bond at all between the Uncles and Alex as they were all football mad and Alex had no interest in sport of any kind. He was a species that they could not understand as Alex was quiet and retiring and possibly excessively shy but when he spoke on any subject he had good ideas which were well expressed. As he grew to maturity the Uncles would defer to him without a mention of football. So he had outstripped them all and their scorn had turned to admiration.

Mary's husband Willie worked in the Singer Sewing Machine factory from boyhood to manhood. Their house was in Clydebank, just above the McAlpine houses called The Holy City because of their flat roofs. I loved visiting them travelling leisurely along on the top floor of the tramcar. It was a run in the country as we travelled on the open topped tram through stretches of parkland from Partick……………….. Regretfully Bessie's story is unfinished due to her last illness and subsequent death in August 1973. She was greatly missed by all the family and many friends.

Most of her story she set out to tell was completed but I feel (daughter Nancy), that she would have been pleased that I have tried to put an ending to her lovely story and I am delighted to do this as best I can.

The notes of her story were handed to me by her on umpteen pieces of all sorts of paper which Alastair managed to sort out and put on his computer (full credit to him). He was ill with Multiple Sclerosis at the time and I think it gave him something to do as he was always a bit of a workaholic. I have used his computer notes to copy this story on to my new Lap Top at 85 years young.

Alastair died in February 1991, after putting up a very brave battle, at the age of 67years.

I will continue to refer to my mum as Bessie as, after all, it is 'Bessie's Story'.

Bessie finished her story at her sister Mary's wedding which leaves Alex who never married although he met a girl when he was serving as a submariner during World War 1. His mother Annie Hunter unfortunately had other ideas and when he was away on duty on the subs told the girl that Alex had a responsibility to his mother who was a lone parent and more or less from what I have heard told her to get lost which was a rotten thing to do. This does not seem like the same strong woman that I remember but I think in those days a son was expected to look after his mother and he would be earning a good wage as a submariner.

Alex never fully forgave her when he heard what she had done and their relationship remained strained.

I now come to Bessie and Tom's wedding and they were married in 1921 a few years after the Great War ended. Tom was lucky to survive this horrible war more or less unscathed, as he served a full four years. He did not talk about his experiences very much but I do know that he saw some horrible sights during that time. He just said that he was one of the lucky ones. His luck still held out when his house was bombed during the Clydebank blitz as a stick of bombs narrowly missed our house and left it uninhabitable. He and I were alone in the house with our dog Dan. Apart from Dan, who was knocked out, we only had cuts and bruising. Once again he just thought we were one of the lucky ones.

Bessie and Tom's Wedding Reception probably went along the same lines as Mary and Willie's, being held in their house in the Gorbals with her mother doing the catering.

Tom was a bookbinder and Bessie a cinema projectionist during the silent films where a pianist played along with the film, fast or slow, according to what was showing on the screen. A bit hilarious !!!! Of course she had to give up her work in the cinema when she got married as married women were not allowed to work in those days – expected to work in the kitchen. Such a waste of training and experience!

They had three children quite quickly, Tom who died at eight months from Whooping Cough, Alastair one year and eight months after Tom and Nancy (me) one year and eight months after Alastair. They must have found out how to put a stop to that as the breeding finished there! Tom did tell Bessie that he would like six children but I will not repeat what she said to that, more or less telling him that he had married the wrong woman.

They lived in a room and kitchen house in Edgefauld Road in Springburn having to haul a pram up several flights of stairs as lots of people had to do then. From there they moved to Bilsland Drive in Ruchill which was a semidetached prefabricated type of house, probably built after the First World War which had a living room, two bedrooms, kitchen and bathroom which were all on the ground floor. There was also a fair sized garden enjoyed by Tom who became a keen gardener.

The next house was in Danes Drive Scotstounhill moving there in 1934. It was a newly built house with two bedrooms upstairs; living room, bathroom and small kitchen downstairs and we had electricity for the first time. All the houses they lived in were rented as only the very well off owned their own houses.

Annie Hunter, Bessie's mother and my granny, came to live with Bessie in Danes Drive during the 1940's her memory was failing and she could no longer live by herself. As a Suffragette in bygone days and also a strong minded person this was a complete reversal and quite sad. We did not have a large house but just had to make the best of things.

Bessie as you can imagine was struggling with food rationing and we all had to be careful but of course Granny Hunter remembered nothing about wars or rationing and pilfered our rations when she got the opportunity. She had a good appetite. Bessie had to devise a method of hiding the rationed food as she would eat a butter ration in the one sitting. It was certainly a very stressful time for Bessie but Granny was eventually admitted to the Southern General Hospital. She died in the late 1940's.

During and after the war years Bessie was very actively involved with the Labour Party and Co-operative Movement and at Election times we all helped with distributing leaflets etc.

Amateur Dramatics was also a pursuit of hers and she frequented the Citizen's Theatre regularly with her friend Mrs. McCaffrey

As a member of her local Co-operative Guild she produced plays and they rehearsed in their houses during the blackout of the war years. This interest helped many of the members of the Guild to get through trying times such as rationing, queuing for food etc. and the fact that many of the ladies had sons and husbands serving abroad in a lot of danger and not knowing if they were safe or not. They all agreed that it was a life saver. A concert was held annually in whatever hall was available.

Bessie's marriage was affected because of her activities as Tom believed that women should be happy to stay at home looking after the family but Bessie once said that when Alastair and I grew up she would live a fuller life and that is just what she did. She would have been most unhappy tied to the house. I think she was born 100 years too soon! Just a pity that Tom could not have accepted things as most other men did – I felt there was a bit of jealousy. She looked after us all well which was not easy in such times, I think she deserved a medal but purely my opinion.

There was talk of a split but this would not have been possible financially so they stuck together going their own ways because there was no other choice. As they grew older they seemed more amenable.

Bessie died in August 1973 from cirrhosis of the liver which puzzled us greatly as she was not a drinker as such. She was quite ill six months before she died with what seemed like flu but refused to see a doctor and said that she would 'doctor' herself with paracetamol. She always had a supply in the house as she was prone to headaches (maybe migraine). In those days there were no warnings to say they could be harmful as we know now.

She spoke to me before she died and said that she wished a private funeral with only the family there and no one from the Labour Party was to be there. I never knew why she had this change of heart as she had spent much of her life supporting them but we respected her wishes. Many of her friends lined up outside the house as the hearse left which I thought was nice.

Tom died three years later in 1976. His sight had failed but true to his generation he coped in his own house with the help of family and a very good neighbour, Jack Reid who kept a keen eye on him.

Despite the constraints of marriage in those times, Bessie fulfilled her ambitions, when the family was off her hands. No one could ask for more.

The ending to Bessie's story was not as she had planned but I have done my best to fill in the remainder of her life as I remember it.

She enjoyed following her projects when family commitments were less as she always said she would and was a superb mother and grandmother. Thanks mum. xxxx

As a postscript to Bessie's, my mum's story and her memory, my perspective must be recorded about the story Alastair's daughter Anne Chambers told me about Bessie possibly being an alcoholic. This astounded me as no one knew my mum better than me .It seems Anne and her sisters were staying with their gran overnight and had been rifling in her dressing table and found alcohol. Apart from the fact that even as children they should not have been doing this I doubt their story. When I cleared out Bessie's possessions I came on quarter bottle of Brandy unopened but assumed she had won it at one of her Labour Party functions and thought no more about it. Because of her strained relationship with Tom all her items were kept in her bedroom. She died of Cirrohsis of the Liver and this may have led to the . assumption but

our doctor was sure she had overdosed on Paracetamol as the dangers were becoming known at that time Three large bottles of Paracetamol were in her dressing table drawer when I cleared out her belongings and I know she took them regularly for headaches. My mum stayed with us for two weeks before go
ing into hospital and she had a very lucid mind and knew she was dying which was hard on us.
It is so mindless to feel I have to justify that my mum was no alcoholic. She had a difficult time with Tom and shortage of money and certainly none for alcohol. Eight months before she died she had a serious illness like flu but would not see a doctor and of course treated herself with Paracetamol. From that time she gradually went downhill dying in Gartnavel Hospital.
I was close to mum and nursed her through her final illness and up to the last few weeks she was an alert caring person with many friends who regarded her well so put her to rest with those thoughts.

.

Nancy
I came on an old type written story by Bessie which was probably written at her writer's class in Glasgow University which I feel is well worth recording even though it is a bit tattered it is still legible. I will tell it as she has written it down.

" The daffodil tractor danced joyfully over the half acre plot, swerving, deviating, gyrating as it levelled the ground for the concrete columns that would rise to fix a rigid glare on diminutive human beings beneath. It seemed such a tiny patch of ground to have sheltered fifty families in the demolished building, families who had wrested so courageously to win from life a bare existence in a period when social conscience had not been shamed from indifference.

They were drawn together in various degrees of poverty where the effort to conceal surpassed the struggle to defeat it. Families from the Highlands, the Borders, the Hebrides and Ireland and several Jewish families who had fled from one of the pogroms in Russia. In the course of time this blend of mankind humanised the ugly tenement with a warmth of fellowship that flowered in the homely sharing of each other's hardships. In the city of their adoption the dawn song that awakened them was the clatter of workmen's heavy boots on the twisting stairs as the men dashed off to the nearby shipyards for a 6 am start with pockets bulging with 'pieces' that sustained them till 6 pm. The homes they had left were the two apartment type, four to the landing in a four storey tenement with no hot water and lavatories were outside. Before the men were off to work the day had already started for the women and tasks were titanic. Fuel for the fire, food in the pots, children to school, emery to clean steel, babies to breast feed, scrubbing clothes, scrubbing floors, sewing new clothes from old. Dungarees to wash, not forgetting nappies which were usually pieces of torn off sheet. Hurly beds had also to be put away beneath beds Heads had also to be braided which took time Visits to tickshop and pawnshop also a chore. A jungle of human wants shrieking for attention and from this primitive material with its greedy demands closely united families were fashioned with influences for good reaching out to the community beyond.. Every experience of life took place within that building. There was Mrs Howieson who brought all the babies into the world, a widow who earned her living stitching servant's wrappers for a warehouse at a few shillings per dozen. The fashion of the period with its long wide skirts, boned bodices with row upon row of hooks and eyes which strained the eyes and fingers was very taxing and she hated it but being a machinist to trade she had to continue to support her family. The side line of midwifery added little to her income but she loved the work and the gratitude of the poverty stricken mothers was her reward. In those days there was no ante natal care, no doctor in attendance and no maternity benefit the women trusting to nature to see them through, but there were many motherless children to disclose how often Mother Nature failed. Every new baby plunged the family deeper into poverty but the touching helplessness of the new born baby was its strength, evoking affectionate and protective bonds in the family circle which made sacrifice a joy. Joyful also were the weddings in our building, the couple leaving to be married through a hail of rice and a pack of children yelling 'hard up' anticipating the shower of coppers that would that would pelt them from the cab window. Back home the wedding feast was being laid out in the parlour, neighbours donating tables, chairs, crockery and cutlery in preparation for the many relations and acquaintances who would be gathering for the evening's revelry.

After the meal a tiny space was miraculously cleared for Lancers and Quadrilles to the strains of "The Waddin' O' Lachie MacGraw.

Part 2. Through the Eyes of a Teenager 1939 – 1945

The 3rd of September 1939 was a memorable day in my life as it was the start of World War 2 and at thirteen years of age was just entering what I was told an exciting time of my life. If nothing else six years surviving a world war brought out a strength and independence in me I may not have had as we got on with life as best we could or stay in the comfort zone of our house and be miserable. No choice there. I know that all the mums of teenagers like me must have had a very hard time setting us free at such a time.

.I lived in Glasgow and my memories are of Mum and Dad saying 'not again'. Dad had come through the 1914-18 war only twenty years previously and to him it seemed such a short time ago. I was partly scared and partly excited but mostly scared about the danger ahead. In the months leading up to the 3rd September we had known that the Germans had invaded countries in the Continent of Europe and of their grim treatment in those countries I had no liking for Germans because of the propaganda and at my age could not distinguish between ordinary Germans and the Nazis.

The war in Japan did not have the same effect on me because it was so distant but some of our friends served in the armed forces there and had some shocking stories to tell when they came home The Japanese forces were much more brutal than the Germans, some of the stories told by returning soldiers really unbelievable The ones who returned home were the lucky ones as many died from the brutality suffered in prison camps and not from bombs and bullets.

It had been a lovely autumnal day on Sunday 3rd September 1939 and in the evening some of our neighbours gathered in the street still in shock but trying to come to terms with the implications of our country at war. We all felt certain it would come as we had been issued with Anderson shelters and gas masks and also advised on the action to take if we were bombed or were invaded by the Germans. Mercifully we were not invaded although from what we have been told it was a close call and we can only by relieved it did not happen or life would be so different.

All houses and business premises had to be blacked out and dad made shuttering for all our windows but we soon got used to it and became part of our lives at war. Street lighting had to be dimmed also so very dull streets making walking hazardous. No house lights shining in the dark either but we became used to it in time and carried torches which also had to be dimmed s. A battery for your torch was not always easy to get as most of those items went to the armed forces. In the forties we had thick black fog sometimes during the winter months as most houses had coal fires which caused the fog so between that and the blackout it was impossible to find your way around. Important to say that tramcars ran a kind of service during those times usually with the conductor walking in front with a lamp. Almost quicker to walk home. Wardens roamed the streets during blackout hours roaring 'put out that light' if there was even a chink of light shown. Some of the wardens felt all important with their new found authority but the pompous ones were soon put in place..

Iron railings round our gardens were removed to be melted down and built into tanks and guns so helping the war effort. We were fortunate to have a privet hedge so our garden was still protected. We were asked to donate pots and pans and any other metal which could be re-used. Air raid sirens sounded occasionally but nothing happened and we even became off hand about them. The odd German plane would come over to take photographs and then make for home but no bombs.

The south coast of England came in for more attention from German bombers than we in Scotland did so in that respect we were lucky.

Schools closed when war was declared and many children were evacuated to safer areas but at age thirteen I did not feel the wish to be evacuated and mum was of the same opinion her feelings being that we should stay together as a family. My biggest regret was losing school friends and the abrupt end to my school days. Friends were scattered far and wide so it was impossible to keep in touch with them. No mobile phones in those days. After a few weeks our school met in a large house in Verona Avenue which the government had taken over but there was little organisation and we were left to our own devices so we know what the outcome of that would be.

On reaching my fourteenth birthday I left school and got an office job in the centre of Glasgow also attending a College in the evening for secretarial work. Schools opened again in a matter of months but I was settled by this time and reasonably happy so life carried on.

Dad worked in a printing firm making cards for birthdays and anniversaries but they were soon taken over by the government and were making armaments for the forces so he had to look for other employment as he had no wish to work in a munitions factory. He figured that he had done his bit in the 1914-18 war. Mum was at home sorting out Ration Books and coping with the food shortages which were to come. Women like mum who stayed at home coping with rationing and never ending queues for food and turning out decent meals were never fully appreciated. Very few had fridges so shopping had to be done each day with a queue at each individual shop, butchers, fruit, fish and grocers as supermarkets where everything could be bought under the same roof were not on the agenda at that time. Few had private cars so after the laborious shopping they had to carry all the shopping home and I have so much admiration for them now which I never had in the 1940's.

Conscription for the armed forces was well under way by 1939 and all healthy young men who were not in a reserved occupation were liable for call up. Some men were conscientious objectors and did not approve of fighting so they were given jobs in the coalmines or in agriculture. As in the 1914-1918 war women took over many of their jobs and proved very capable. There was also the women's services, ATS (Army), WRNS (Navy) and WAAFS (Air Force). The WRNS was the most popular of the services possibly because the uniform was the smartest. It was more difficult to become a Wren so the ones who were successful were inclined to be rather snooty.

Being in the coal industry I was considered to be in a reserved occupation but in the early days of the war I was underage for any of the services. I did get my calling up papers when I was nineteen but the war ended soon after so I never heard any more about it..

Bananas and lemons were no longer available as the war dragged on and food was also affected but with a little thought we came up with some remarkable recipes. Dried egg from America replaced eggs more or less as we were lucky to get one or two eggs per week. It was amazing how we adapted to dried egg and we were still using it years after the war ended. I found it difficult to return to cracking an egg as I had little experience of it. Dried egg and a little of the cheese ration mixed together with milk made a palatable scrambled egg. Carrot in a sponge cake was used long before we had heard of Carrot Cake as it is known to-day. Fish and Chip shops remained open so we could buy a bag of chips or fish supper but they closed early if supplies ran out. Restaurants also got a special supply of food if you had the money to dine out which was rare for our family. My idea of a night out was going to my friend's house and making piles of chips in her kitchen. Her Gran had a wee corner shop and they were never short of basic food. We made our chips with dripping fat and they were totally gorgeous and I have never tasted chips like them since. It has to be taken into account that our diet was seriously lacking in fat so although this would be frowned upon now at that time it was acceptable. Oven chips are a poor substitute but times have changed because of high fats in our food now.

Bread was a staple part of the diet but during the war years it was a very dark colour and not appetising looking but like lots of things we got used to it and it always seemed to be available. From my memory before the war there was a plain loaf which had black and white c rusts and a pan loaf all unsliced so a good breadknife was a must. The fancy loaves we have now had not been created. Vitamins were added to the wartime bread for health reasons because of the shortages in other areas. We were a healthy enough nation after the war with few obese people so it must have worked. The only way we got potato crisps was by making them ourselves which I did occasionally. Mum was a great scone maker so when she had enough rations we enjoyed this treat but as the fat content was low they had to be eaten that day which was no problem. Tinned fruit was quite rare so we appreciated it when available usually after standing an hour in a queue for one wee tin. The same applied to tinned salmon which I do not remember having often. Tinned peaches and Carnation milk were the perfect treat! My brother who was an apprentice engineer received extra bread and meat because he was a
 manual worker but unlike me he said he was always hungry but that was a typical teenager.
The night of March 13th 1941 was a chapter in my life not to be forgotten as the long awaited air raids came to our area. I was in a local cinema with my friend Margaret when an announcement was made that the air raid sirens had sounded. The film was well under way so we decided to wait and see the remainder of the film as air raid sirens were a part of our lives now but usually came to nothing. Before long we could

hear gun fire and as the noise increased we became more nervous. Probably about 9pm we crossed over to the railway station to make our way home and before long a train pulled in. The journey of two stations to our destination was scary as there was complete darkness apart from a full moon and we could see German planes quite clearly
 but as two fifteen hear olds we thought if we got home all would be well such is the innocence of the young. We separated when we got off the train and that was the last I saw of my friend for ten long months.
Dad and our dog were alone in the house so he was pleased to see me but my brother was at Evening Classes in the local school and mum was in town no doubt at one of her political meetings. Within about an hour the raid became very alarming with bombs falling but I found it difficult to distinguish between gun fire and bombs. We sheltered in a cupboard in the kitchen which dad had rigged out for an occasion such as this. The noise was quite horrendous and our dog was petrified but I held on to him tightly to calm him and my
 legs were scratched with his claws. If I had not been so scared myself I would have been sorry for him but I truly thought that we would all die in that cupboard the noise was so dreadful We had anti-aircraft guns nearby on Anniesland Road and they were very noisy and scary and cracked some windows before the bombs finished them off with most of the house..
A stick of three bombs landed near us one of them just outside the kitchen we were sheltering in The rear of the house caved in on us but the cupboard we were in withstood

most of the blast. Once we came to and realised we seemed unhurt except for plaster in the mouth, ears and nose and still a racket going on outside we had to consider how to get out. Dad gave good advice and told me to keep still in case any other part of the house fell on us. Where the kitchen window had been was our exit place so we clambered over loads of rubble and out to the rear of the house beside a huge bomb crater. We soon realised that there was no dog, we called him but there was no response so assumed he was dead and we knew we would have to find other shelter till things quietened down. We found later that the cupboard we were in was the only item standing in the kitchen as it had been protected by a large iron oven shielding us from the blast of the bomb so our family history could have been very different.

We were all safe that night including our dog crawling out from the rubble a few hours later wagging his tail when he heard our voices. I cried when I saw him and also the fact that my mum had partly walked home from her meeting. I was so pleased to see her alive and well. We were not a demonstrative family but on that occasion I gave mum a silent hug for being in one piece.

Only a few hours earlier Margaret and I left for the cinema leaving a pleasant area and now it seemed in ruins and in some ways not recognisable but most of our residents survived so we had to appreciate that.

The following afternoon when trying to rescue some items of clothing from our bombed house an aircraft appeared and drew a swastika in the sky also saying 'we will be back to-night'.

It was very scary knowing what we had gone through the previous night but as it turned out the raid was not as prolonged as the night before but we were exhausted and longing for a sleep. We got lodgings with friends of my parents who lived in the area and their house was undamaged apart from a few broken windows. We stayed with them for ten months until our own house was made habitable again. The loss of life on Clydeside those two nights was shocking and most people knew many who were dead or badly injured. It was common for people to be dug out of buildings a week to ten days after the raids and they survived. We gradually returned to a way of living but I was once more separated from my friends and missed them a lot but that was the way it was and glad to be alive. One of Winston Churchill's many quotes was "When you go through hell keep walking" That was the therapy given out in the 1940s and maybe we could do with more of it now. After what seemed a life time to me we returned to our repaired house with white cloth for windows as glass was in short supply. This seemed strange at first but like everything else we had to adapt to it. We got extra clothing coupons for clothes we had lost and also points and financial assistance to buy new furniture. Being sixteen I was delighted with my new bedroom.

Normality gradually returned and my best friend and I picked up our life again, mainly Ballroom Dancing twice a week and the cinema which we loved. They were mostly American films with fabulo us dresses which we envied and Margaret received magazines from relatives in Canada which we read avidly longing for all the lovely clothes and make-up. We had to queue for hours at Boots the Chemist when make-up was delivered and word got around very fast when any supplies came in. We had a way of melting down the end bits of lipstick and making them into a full tube again. Shade did not particularly matter and it was a bit of a gamble waiting to see if it was a reasonable colour. The same applied to soap which was really basic and no great choice. We made a container from chicken wire and put all the small pieces of soap we had saved into it and when it was shaken about the water it made suds. Dad made us a super model of the container which lasted us throughout the war.

Bombing became less after the severe raids of 1941 and although we still had nights in shelters because of the air raid sirens no bombs fell near us. Greenock was a target and the German's notion was to wipe out the shipyards which did not happen in spite of the damage to them. Bad news was kept from the public so we never knew the true facts. There was no alternative but to carry on with living and we did reasonably well in hindsight. London was the main target for air raids and they had months of continuous bombing which must have been ghastly.

One man who scared me so much was Lord Haw-Haw who broadcast most nights from Germany calling "Germany Calling, Germany Calling" in the most menacing voice. Dad listened to him avidly but I tried to avoid listening if I could. He assured us we were losing the war and it would be just a matter of time before the Germans came so we should surrender now or we would be bombed into oblivion. His voice was unforgettable and spine chilling but he was executed after the war and good riddance.

In 1942 I met George at the Albert Ballroom in Glasgow which was by far the most likely place to meet your partner in the 1940's Pubs were a no go area for my age group although we did have the oc
casional visit for one tiny drink but I never really enjoyed the atmosphere. Big bands were in vogue and in ballrooms there would be about fifteen to twenty musicians making up the band so the music was huge and add to that the dancing which made a great evening. Must not forget the talent that was there The floor was crowded to capacity most nights and more males to females because of the Forces so a good time for us girls. There were two or three very large ballrooms in Glasgow and they attracted the big bands like Joe Loss and Glen Millar but we preferred the smaller venues The American service men or GI's as they were better known took over the centre of Glasgow or perhaps it just seemed they did as they were so loud and confident Their uniforms were made of the best material as only the Americans can do but certain girls idolized them and enjoyed their confident charm plus the fact that they had loads of nylon stockings to hand out and sweets and chocolate but they also tossed sweets to children in the passing so credit there. There were many unwanted babies and also GI Brides when the GI's finally left and some of the brides did not find things as they expected when they got to America and many returned to Britain after sampling the hardships of farm life in the back of beyond. Some of the GI's spun yarns about life with Mom

and Dad back in the USA which turned out to be a lot of fiction. Our American cousins were very plausible to some trusting girls in Britain. The few that I came across were long winded and intent in talking about themselves but I suppose there must have been nice ones also.

My teenage years spent during a world war were relatively carefree and happy although the uncertainty of our existence was never far away but we had great times as well as bad which applies to most teenagers of all generations. Obstacles were there to overcome and my memories of that particular time of my life are that we enjoyed every minute of our teenage years but would love to have been able to buy more clothes and make up. Living through such times was hard but probably character building also so no long lasting effect that I know of.

Knitting was common place with young and old and as wool was in short supply we unravelled old sweaters, ripped them out, put the wool in hanks and after washing it was almost like new. No article of clothing was thrown out as dresses and skirts were unpicked and made into new items When turned inside out the material was like new. I fortunately had a friend who was extremely good at dressmaking. Ripping ot sweaters continued for some time after clothing coupons had ceased to exist as we had become accustomed to this way of living and found it hard to throw clothing away. The 'throw away' society was far into the future in the 1940s and 50s. Dad was an expert at repairing our shoes and when we got new shoes he stuck on a rubber sole to prolong their life. This continued long after the war finished and even after I was married.

Each day there were recipes on the radio (wireless then) to help cope with rationing. One of them I remember was Woolton Pie named after the minister of food. It contained only vegetables with a pie topping and really tasted nice but the crust was quite hard because of the lack of fat in the pastry. If you were lucky enough to get a lemon or orange every part of it was used, the skin being grated to put on top of puddings or cakes. My mum used the rind of such fruit till the day she died it was routine to her.

George and I were having a very happy-go-lucky life as only teenagers can do dancing as may times a week as we could afford and cinema visits living in our own tiny world until 1944 when he unexpectedly got his 'calling up' papers. He was always of the opinion that he was in a reserved occupation serving his time in engineering. We both were shocked out of our make believe world so off he went to do his bit for King and country. He landed in god forsaken Fort George for eight weeks hard training to make some kind of soldier of him then was posted to the Royal Corp of Signals where he served from 1945 – 1948 doing most of his time in Egypt. It was also a difficult time for me adjusting to being on my own again but I continued dancing a few times a week and joined a dramatic club in Clydebank and more or less got on with my life. Bombing in Glasgow was not a problem now and apart from scarcities we were trying to return to normal but 'normal' for me would not return till George came home. Each time he had leave and was away for another year the world stopped spinning such are the intensities of youth..

May 1945 saw the war in Europe ending to the great relief of everyone. The six years of war seemed like a lifetime to me but the relief was huge and it took some time for the fact to sink in. Most people gathered in the streets to celebrate and I walked with some friends to Clydebank which had suffered greatly in the air raids but it was gradually dragging itself back to some sort of normality. My friends were residents of Clydebank and were lucky to have survived the Blitz in 1941 which flattened their town. Everyone was your friend on VE (victory in Europe) day and I have never known a mood like it. We still had years of rationing and scarcities ahead but no-one cared on VE day' The war in the Far East finished with the atomic bomb in August of that year which was a gruesome affair but at the time we were glad the fighting was over with the prospect of peace and soldiers returning home. The shocking atrocities of Hitler's concentration camps and death camps had still to unfold which proved to be an appalling chapter in history. Their story has been written about on many occasions and it is still difficult to grasp how humanity could sink so low.

This is the story of war years during my teens from bits that I remember and over all I have great memories and also nasty ones and although I would not like to go through it again I don't think

it has had any lasting repercussions. One thing that remains with me and will continue to do so is the smell of plaster when decorating and my mouth full of it in 1941 when the bombs fell.

It never fails to amaze me that human beings can come through such terrifying times with the constant fear of bombing and death yet manage to live a fairly normal life and actually find some enjoyment and happiness along with the horrors.

Margaret and I met Archie and George, who were cousins during this traumatic time and eventually married so something good came out of it all. George and I were married for sixty five years and he died aged ninety one so we had a good life. Sadly he had memory loss in the last years of his life which was difficult to deal with but we got through it and he will always be in our hearts.

Part 3. Nancys Story

Developing arthritis at the age of 85 years and becaming less able to get around , life sort of closed in on me so I had to take other roads to keep myself sane (my brain seems o.k. at the moment). The idea of writing an account of my life came to me as I had just completed the story of my mother's life from where she had left off when she died. Her story was of great interest to me as I learned more about her than when she was alive. She had attended a Literary Class at Glasgow University when she was in her sixties and it was suggested there that she write a story about her life in the Gorbals She enjoyed many happy years at this Class and it was such a pity that she did not complete her story. This encouraged me to write my own story so I'm sure that my mum would have been very pleased. Sheila and Lesley hopefully will add their wee bit and keep the ball rolling!.

I was born on the 6th November 1925 at 2p.m. during a ten day period of thick black fog caused by all the smokey chimneys that were around in those day. My Gran was in attendance in our house at Edgefauld Road, Springburn Doctors were only called in extreme circumstances as it was rather costly.

My father named me Annie after my Gran but my mum decided to call me Nancy as she did not like the name Annie. This has caused a bit of confusion in my life at times!.

My father was a Bookbinder/Printer to trade and spent his early working days in McCorkindale's the printers. My mother was a Cinema Projectionist in the days of silent films at a Cinema in the George's Cross area. She must have earned a fairly good wage but unfortunately married women were not allowed to work which seems an awful waste of training. Things have changed for the better since the 1920's.

My brother Alastair was 1 year 8 months old when I was born – only a baby himself. I think he may have resented me for as mum said 'he was an awkward wee devil'. My other brother Tom was born first but died from whooping cough at eight months old.

Quite a tragedy for my parents.

Most working class people lived in tenement buildings or flats as they are known now, and mostly one room and kitchen flats with a toilet on the stair. Prams had to be hauled up and down stairs which was no mean feat. No worries about getting the pounds off after childbirth. Owning a car was very unusual in our area so shopping had to be done on 'Shank's Pony'. The word 'obese' was rarely used as were 'going to the Gym'.

There was no electricity in our house so no vacuums even had we been able to afford them, so all housework had to be done with a wee hand brush (down on the knees). Laundry was done in a single black sink, all water having to be heated. A fire had to be cleaned out and lit each day and coal brought in from wherever, probably a cupboard in the stair or in the house. There were no Radios Televisions ot Telephones (such hardship) I think I'll go and have a wee seat now!

For all the hard manual work that had to be done Alastair and I were taken to Springburn Park most days to feed the ducks etc. This was important to my mum to get out of the house and in the fresh air. She was not a house proud person and could leave a bit of dust around without having a nervous breakdown. The 'dust gene' was passed on to me.

We moved to Bilsland Drive in Ruchill when I was two years of age to a wooden semi detached cottage type house built after the first world war. This must have been a step up for my parents as there was a garden which dad had a passion for. The house was opposite Ruchill Hospital , a fever hospital for all infectious diseases which were widespread at that time. When I was about seven or eight my chum and I spent some time at the hospital gates chatting to the Gatehouse Keepers who occasionally allowed us to help them open the gates to let the ambulances through. We seemed to have a fascination for the ambulances and the people in them. We had no thought for infection as there must have been plenty bugs around.

The lamplighter who came round to light the gas lamps in the streets was also a friend of ours as he always had sweeties. He would probably be arrested now for talking to us which is a pity because he was a lovely man.

While staying in Bilsland Drive we acquired a puppy – I was scared of a dog called Sandy who stayed a few doors away from us. It seemed to wait for me coming home from school and would dive at me barking like mad leaving me petrified till mum saved me. She did assure me that Sandy was really quite friendly but I was not convinced. Mum's thoughts were that if I owned a dog from a puppy I would get over this fear. I think it helped because I loved Dan to bits – but still hated Sandy!

Dan came from an elderly Aunt of Dad who was called Danielena McSporran – that was really her name! Dan was named after her and he was a real street dog but very affectionate. He lived a good life till he was thirteen years of age when he had to be put down because of illness. When our house was bombed in 1941 Dan was injured by a brick to his head but survived intact apart from his sight deteriorating. Dogs have a strong sense of smell so this compensates for sight loss so I'm told.

My school years began in Ruchill School, a three storey red sandstone building. On my way to school that first day I asked mum how long I would be at school and she replied 'till you are fourteen' which was leaving age at that time. My heart fell to my feet as I thought I was away for nine years which made for a very unhappy first day at school. Alastair was reluctantly brought in to try and console me.

Sand trays were handed out at school, which as it sounds were trays filled with sand and we wrote our letters and numbers on them and shook them to make them disappear again. I loved them so things began to look up at school for me. I often wonder what the kids of to-day would do with them! From sand trays we progressed to slates which squeaked when written on – must have driven the teacher mad. We finally progressed to pencils and jotters.

A fire started in the basement of our school one day which caused some excitement especially among the teachers who kept telling us to remain calm but from what I can remember we enjoyed seeing the Fire Engines arrive and all the excitement. It also surprised me how quickly our mothers appeared on the scene, news spreading quickly no doubt as most of us lived fairly close to the school. We had a few days off school so that was good.

Dad bought a lovely new motor bike and sidecar about this time from money left in a will by a relative who lived in America. Our holidays were spent touring England, which seemed like a foreign country to me, mostly camping but if we were lucky Bed and Breakfast.

Most Sundays, in the summer months, we met up with friends who also had motor bikes – the Phillips who had a son and daughter and the Blaneys who also had a son and daughter. We motored into the 'country', built a fire and had a picnic (smokey tea). The funny thing is that the weather always seemed to be sunny – memory lapse here! I doubt if mum really enjoyed being rattled around in the motor bike, don't think it was her choice but dad loved it so end of story. I got a nasty burn on my leg from the exhaust pipe when I was eight years old. We were in Leeds at the time and had to hunt for a chemist to get burn dressings. It probably required hospital treatment as it was very painful but parents treated their children when accidents happened and we survived. I have still a mark on my leg but it has moved further up.

We were members of a Camping Association who were based at East Kilbride which was then in the heart of the countryside. Our tent was very large and completely waterproof with a wooden floor, rugs etc. Two double beds were to the rear of the tent, a dresser, table and four folding chairs were at the front of the tent with cooking facilities such as primus stove and a paraffin stove which was probably highly dangerous but no accidents that I remember!

Mum did all the cooking of course but Alastair and I had to fetch the water in pails over a field with cows in it which I did not like. Most of the water must have spilled by the time we got back as they were quite heavy.

Weekends and school holidays were spent at East Kilbride with dad appearing at weekends on the motor bike of course. It was quite a large camp with plenty of chums and things to do and my parents made life long friends. Bakers, Butchers, Fish and Fruit vans called at the gate with eggs and milk supplied by the farmer. There were no 'ready meals' so mum cooked everything on those two stoves.

Now and again we walked the two miles into the village of East Kilbride (mum loved walking).

It was a change to see different shops I suppose but Alastair and I did not like the walk and probably sulked a bit.

There was a time during this walk on the way back that mum handed Alastair and I a stick and she had a much larger one. It seems that there was a suspicious looking man sitting on a seat at the side of the road. She told us to use it if necessary which puzzled us as mum was very pacifist in her ways. We were told to do as she says and walk smartly behind her. We must have scared the guy for he never budged as we passed. We never found out what he was up to but one can guess now! Mum certainly would have defended her young pacifist or not! That episode added to the interest of the walk although we never knew the full story.

For two weeks in July every year during Glasgow Fair Fortnight where almost all places like shipyards and businesses closed down leaving Glasgow deserted, we went to the Clarion Camp at Catacol Bay, Lochranza, Arran.

Pre-war about 100 attended the Camp which consisted of people of all ages some quite elderly. I enjoyed it as there were plenty of children my own age who, like myself, came each year. A huge marquee was erected where we ate all our meals from trestle tables and form type seats. A chef was employed and a rota of campers assisted each day. The food was plain but seemed to be plenty of it. There was a sweetie shop in the camp run by a rota of members also so we could always buy extras.

Concerts were held in the marquee fairly regularly at night time and the usual people who were keen performed, some good, some bad. Mine was usually singing or dancing – probably bad. Alastair hated all this and I found out quite recently that he did not like the camp at all and never returned to Arran after his teen years. He loved cycling and staying in a wee crawl in tent in the Glencoe area, not my scene at all. He had friends who liked the same things as he did and they climbed the mountains in the Glencoe area.

Mum was Secretary and dad Treasurer of the Camp for many years (too many probably) but it was always difficult to encourage people to take up those positions and mum and dad seemed to enjoy doing it anyway. Some people referred to it as Tom and Bessie's Camp.

During the war years the numbers shrunk to a mere 20 or so and no chef was employed so all had to muck in. We had our meals in the large hut which was used for cooking and storing tables and seats throughout the year. It was very comfortable and nice and warm when it rained.

The military were stationed all over Arran but it was still an idyllic spot to be during the war years , very peaceful and cut off from the rest of the world. Newspapers and radios were not allowed in the camp for the 2 weeks so we lived in our own wee space. There was one exception when a warship appeared in Catacol Bay just overlooking the camp and began firing practice. The noise echoed through the hills and it was ear splitting. Poor Dan was petrified and mum took him a walk up a valley where the noise was less frightening. Being in my teens the Dances held in the Lochranza Town hall three times per week were the highlight of the holiday. There were no shortages of partners due to the military presence so it suited the females. We had a two mile walk from Catacol to Lochranza and about six of us did this walk with the return journey mostly done in our bare feet walking on the grass edge. It was agreed beforehand that we would all return together (and we did!)

In pre-war days we sailed from the Broomielaw in Glasgow on either the Dalriada or Davaar – two quite small ships which also carried cargo. The destination was Cambeltown but we left the ship at Lochranza which was a six hour sail from Broomielaw. No alcoholic drink on board and we carried our own sandwiches and tea so arrived absolutely sober! No singing or entertainment either, just a lovely quiet six hour sail which by the time we reached Greenock was really boring for Alastair and I.

A large trunk was packed with all our clothing and picked up by carrier a week before we sailed. We did not have much to wear during that week. The trunk was dumped at Lochranza Pier and the farmer delivered it to the camp. It never seemed to go missing which was quite fortunate. The trunk came back the same way with all the soiled clothing which poor mum had to wash by hand, sunlight soap and scrubbing board, a hard life. Thus ends the story of our many holidays in Arran.

My Gran (mother's mother) moved to Torrance from Sandbank in Dunoon -
 I do not know exactly when but I was quite young and my memories are of a fairly large house with big front garden facing the sea. On returning in my adult years I was quite surprised to see a mid terrace sort of ordinary house. Anyway she landed in Torrance as most of you know, and we travelled by motor bike to visit her. Bob, my gran's much loved Irish wolf hound Heinz kind of a dog could hear the bike approaching about a mile away and came to meet us at the start of the village barking all the way in welcome and accompanied us back through the village barking at the wheels back to gran's house. My dad thought he was mad but gran thought he was just a clever wee dog. Remember there was not a lot of traffic about and it must have been a sort of event when we arrived in Torrance – at least Bob made it so! Living on her own gran adored Bob he even shared a place at the table with her. She found him abandoned in West Street stuck to the tar on the road. He was in rather a mess but gran took him home. Dad's reaction was that he would be better to be 'put down' but her reply was that she would rather put him down than the dog – that was how fond she was of animals. She seemed to get the tar off with butter and patiently nursed him back to health (without the aid of a Vet). He was a very faithful dog and lived to a good age.

Dad's parents both died when I was quite young so I have few memories of them. They lived in Lochwinnoch and I only remember my gran being bedridden from what seemed to be a stroke. Granda died from blood poisoning due to an insect bite on his arm. Antibiotics would probably have saved him to-day. They were likely to have been in their late sixties when they died.

When I was nine years old we moved to Scostounhill because
the huts that we lived in Ruchill were being demolished to make way for a housing estate of tenement houses. Dad had to have a garden so the house we moved into was newly built and had a fair size garden. There were two bedrooms upstairs and living room, kitchen and bathroom downstairs. The living room had a coal fire and sheer joy we had electricity. Just to press a switch and light a room seemed magic to us kids.

The motor bike was sold about this time as I was growing too big for the small seat in the sidecar. I don't remember going to East Kilbride when we moved to Scotstounhill so it was not missed in that respect.

Victoria Drive Primary was my new school and was a wooden annexe close to our house. I missed my friends at Ruchill and at nine years old it was a scary thing going to a new school but I crept in to the class of new faces feeling very vulnerable. Miss Chalmers, my new teacher remarked that our names were similar, I was introduced then shown my seat and told to listen carefully and I would soon pick up what was going on in the class – end of story.

On my way home from school at four o'clock I met a girl who lived two doors away from us. Her name was Clarinda and she was a year older than me and by the time we walked home we were on good terms. She had moved to the area recently and was also pleased to meet someone who lived nearby. I really liked the wee wooden school and soon settled in forgetting my chums at Ruchill.

Scotstoun School in Dunglass Avenue was my next school which I moved to in Primary seven because our lovely wee wooden school in Danes Drive was taken over by Victoria Drive Secondary who seemed to have plans for it.

My memories of Scotstoun School were marching up and down stairs to the accompaniment of stirring marches thumped out on the piano in the hall below. We marched in two's and it seemed a successful way of getting children from A to B but somehow don't think it would work with to-day's children!

Many years later when I was in my sixties I and a friend attended Country Dance Spciety Classes in the evening at Scotstoun School. They were very much no nonsense classes and got dirty looks when putting a foot wrong. The year we had there certainly improved our movements but we went back to the classes where we could have a laugh if footwork went wrong leaving Society Classes for those with more technical ambitions.

While walking the dog in Victoria Park I met a friendly teacher collecting leaves for
 her class and when I told her I had attended Scotstoun Schoo lmany years ago she invited me to talk to the kids about my experiences pre war years. She said I would be made very

welcome but I never took up her invite which I feel sorry about.

Coming to live near the River Clyde in the 1930s was very noisy with the liveliness of shipbuilding and all the other associated industries. There was a buzz day and night, hammering and welding and on foggy days during the winter there was the constant hoot of fog horns on the river. During the war years this increased but it is amazing what human beings can get accustomed to and we took no notice of it eventually. No alarm clock was required in the morning as the hooters sounded of at 7.30am at the shipyards and this continued throughout the day at Lunch (then dinner time) and at change of shifts. As age overtakes me and I am at home on my own most of the day the silence is total and my thoughts go back to times gone by. The digital age has come and we must accept change.

From the age of six I attended the William Morris Choir and Dancing Class – eurhythmics to be exact. It was held on a Saturday afternoon in Cuthbertsons the piano shop at the corner of Sauchiehall Street and Cambridge Street where Adams is now and C & A used to be.

We had a wonderful choir master called Mr Houston and I was put in the soprano section. He made singing very enjoyable as he had a lovely personality.

Dancing classes came after an hour of the choir so it lasted all of the afternoon so mum shopped along Sauchiehall Street which was a real shopping area then. We travelled by tramcar from the door of Cuthbertsons to the door of our house in Bilsland Drive.

The usual display was held annually but not the expensive ones held by dancing classes now. Mum made my dresses which were never too elaborate. I gained a liking for singing and dancing in those classes and kept them going till I was about eleven years of age when other pursuits took over.

On Saturday afternoons Alastair was dragged probably unwillingly to watch Partick Thistle play at Firhill as dad was a keen supporter. I can remember when I was very young going to Firhill and watching the game from dad's shoulders. My main interest was the sweeties he bought me.

After passing what was then called 'The Qualifying' (Qualie for short) I progressed to Victoria Drive Secondary School. Having gained enough marks to gain a place in a secondary school was considered the tops. Failing that it was an Advanced Division School which although good was sort of frowned upon (a bit snobby) but that's the way it was. Alastair managed to get top marks when he entered Secondary School but I was further down the scale which did not bother me except for the fact that Alastair's teachers expected me to get good marks also which put on the pressure. They soon found out I was not a genius and left me alone.

I enjoyed my time at secondary school, short though it was. My favourite subjects were French and English and I also enjoyed Science. I was not particularly good at it but we had a smashing looking teacher called Mr Imrie and he made the class very interesting. (just by being there).

Sorry Sheila but hockey was not my scene as my memories of that were being stuck in goal frozen stiff. I liked Tennis and played that a bit after school hours at Scotstoun in the nice warm weather.

We were also taken to Whiteinch Baths once a week and lined up along the pool in a sitting position .Whether you could swim or not the teacher walked along and pushed us all in. I always tried to get the shallow end of the pool. I did not like swimming lessons for obvious reasons.

In my third year at secondary school in 1939 the second world war broke out bringing my education to an abrupt halt overnight. The school was immediately used as a First Aid Centre so our classes were held in a large house in Verona Avenue but we were mainly left to our own devices which did not work at all well. Lots of my friends were evacuated and I missed them. Our family decided to stay together for which I was glad as I would not have been happy being evacuated. The classes at Verona Avenue were quite small and a wide range of ages, sometimes teachers came in and sometimes they did not which also applied to the pupils. All a bit of a disaster really and education practically zero. Schools re-opened after a few months but as I was fourteen I had already left and was working in an office in Queen Street. I attended Skerry's College in Bath Street for Shorthand and Typing twice a week in the evenings

The suddenness of the end of my schooldays and loss of my classmates had quite an effect on me but it was only the beginning of many worse traumas to come our way in the following years so we had to make the best of circumstances..

My first job was for a Furrier in Queen Street when I was fourteen years of age and very green. Most of the day I was left alone as Mr McLashan was out and about seeing customers. On my first day I was petrified and when the phone rang held it upside down (it was one of the old black ones).I can't remember who it was or what I said but I somehow got through it. Looking back it seems a bit daft leaving a young girl alone especially as I had no experience. No work experience in those days! There was also the thousands of beautiful fur coats and capes surrounding me, rail after rail of them. I could have hopped off with the lot but being so young I was not impressed. My one aim was to get through the day in one piece.

Part of my job was to deliver arm loads of furs to the various shops in the centre of Glasgow and that at least got me out of that office/warehouse but I hated the job. Mr McGlashan spoke very little so it was very lonely and after a few weeks I packed it in. My wages there were 10/- per week (old money) My gran said that she worked for a Mr McGlashan in Queen Street in her younger days when she sewed for a living and she reckoned it was the same family which was quite a coincidence.

Next job took me to a coal agent's office in 163 Hope Street, four floors up in a red sandstone building which is still there to-day. There were six staff employed and I came in as the junior working at a small three line switchboard, a bit scary at first but had help from the girl above me, soon learning about how not to cut phone calls off! I was also in SOLE charge of the stamp book (how good can you get) but every stamp had to be entered in a book with a note of the customer and it had to balance at the end of each day which was my first introduction to book-keeping, in a very modest way.

The five years I spent in this office gave me a good grounding for office work as I eventually did typing and more advanced forms of book-keeping eventually taking over from the cashier when she was on holiday which was the icing on the cake. The advantages of a small office are that you have to learn to do everything which no amount of training at College can give you.

Lunch break was one and a half hours so I managed home for my mince and tatties (dinner was mid-day then). I travelled by train from Queen Street station which was cheaper than the bus and

 I always had to take the cheapest route..

I earned extra money by working in the jewellery department of the Clydebank Co-op in Clydebank. I worked a five and a half day week in my regular job in Hope Street so that left Saturday afternoon free Working in a shop did not really appeal to me and the jewellery department was a bit boring so I left within the year. I think I had met George by this time so probably preferred going out with him.

During the 1940's we had to learn to live with severe food rationing, clothes on coupons, fuel scarcities and very few sweets which were also rationed. The blackout was also a depressing feature of the 1940's but somehow we adapted quite well. Face make up was very scarce so we made up our own. We dissolved sugar in hot water and applied it to our hair after washing in order to stiffen it and keep our curls in. It was amazing how many household items were used in different ways. A make do and mend culture came from necessity. Our disposable society of to-day could learn a few things from the 1940's but we hope never to go back to that era and who would really want to? Looking back we did have many happy times probably because we were teenagers and free from most worries but ourselves.

 Many cleaning agents used then are still being used today such as vinegar (not malt) and Soda Crystals.

The 13th March 1941 is a date never to be forgotten by me as it changed our lives so completely and unexpectedly The horror and fear of that night will stay with me forever..
Margaret Kelly and I decided to have a night at the cinema so decided on The Tivoli in Crow Road – I do not even remember what picture was showing that night but we had been in an hour so when the air raid sirens sounded. As this happened fairly often we were not particularly worried and stayed put to see the remainder of the film thinking that it would be another false alarm. Before long it became rather noisy outside with gun fire and what we thought were bombs in the distance so we made for home via Partick railway station which was across the road. As you can imagine it was pitch black outside except for this lovely full moon shining from a lovely clear sky – a bombers moon as it was called. A train appeared before too long also in complete darkness. I must admit we were becoming a bit scared and just wanted to get home as the guns were making quite a din by now and we could hear aeroplanes. Being on a train was not the safest of places as railway lines were inclined to be bombed. We were glad when Scotstounhill station appeared (no-one to collect our tickets)

Little did I know that I would not see my pal for nine months but that was war and full of 'separations' and heartbreak.

We made for home pronto and my dad was waiting at the door as he was in alone and obviously worried about us so he was pleased to see at least one of us. We immediately went into the cupboard in the kitchen which was rigged out as a sort of shelter to protect us from flying glass. There was a long form like seat in it which was about all there was room for so that is where dad, Dan the dog and myself sheltered. Dan was frantic with all the noise and we did our best to pacify him, he sat on my knee shaking like a jelly. (me also). I must admit I was very frightened but dad was, or seemed calm.

After spending about an hour in the cupboard, the noisiest hour I will ever spend, a stick of three bombs fell, one of them in our back garden and the house seemed to be coming down about us, actually the rear half of the house where we were sheltering in the cupboard was pretty well demolished. We sat for a while to make sure nothing else would fall on us then crawled out where the window had been into the still moonlight night. Dan fell off my knee and seemed to be unconscious. We were very shocked but glad to be alive with only cuts and bruises which was incredible when we saw the state of the house. An old fashioned cast iron cooker was between the cupboard we were in and the bomb so it gave us protection from the blast and probably we owe a lot to it. We were choked by debris in our mouths and nose and this seemed to worry me most of all.

The one stable thing through all this was my dad who knew exactly what to do (or so I thought). He took me to an Anderson shelter across the road which my chum Margaret was in. It was packed with people including a driver and conductress of a bus which had fallen into a crater of one of the bombs but they did not seem to be injured. I was desperate for a drink but that was a no go as the water pipes were damaged.

We knew that our neighbours were trapped in their shelter and dad tried to get volunteers to help him dug them out but no one from that shelter budged including our neighbourhood air raid warden who was supposed to be in charge during emergencies. He was too scared to move and said he had to look after his family. As a fifteen year old I never gave my dad much thought but I did admire him that night as he managed to get the injured neighbours out of their shelter and get help at a first aid station down the road at Kingsway. One had a serious head injury from shrapnel and she was only nine years of age. My chum Clarinda also had a back injury but it proved not to be too serious. My opinion of my dad changed that night. There was no help for the walking wounded and you just had to survive by your own devices. I know that dad and I had a special relationship from that day onwards as we were so

 near being blown to bits that night of 13 th March 1941.

Mum was at a meeting of something or other in town and had to walk home from Partick through knee deep debris when a Warden told her that the Scotstounhill housing scheme had been badly hit by bombs Not even Hitler himself would have stopped her trying to get home

. She arrived home about 2a.m. when most of the bombing was in Clydebank. Dad was examining the ruins of his house when she appeared, and she took some convincing that

Alastair and I were safe (Alastair was at Evening Classes in Victoria Drive School so was in their shelter). During the time that my parents were taking in what had happened there was a noise in the rubble of the house and out crawled a very bedraggled Dan. He must have come round and heard my mum's voice so that was a bit of good news. He never fully recovered and as I've said already lived till he was thirteen years but went gradually blind. I cried for spme time when Dan came back from the dead that night. I know he was only a dog and there were so many killed and injured but he was MY dog and merited a few tears of joy among the chaos.

It's worth a mention here that if we had an Anderson shelter it would have been in the garden where the bomb fell and we would have been history and the family tree very different. Dad always said that if we were protected from flying debris we would be as safe as a shelter as nothing would withstand a direct hit with a bomb. How true that was – thanks dad! I am a believer in fate. When our house was made habitable again we did accept a brick shelter in the back garden having seen what glass and flying debris can do but fortunately we did not have to use it and it housed bikes and gardening materials. No one could get me into an airraid shelter after the 13th March 1941 and I have always had a fear of enclosed spaces but who knows if I would have been like that anyway.

In the early hours of that unforgettable morning, with no home, dad, me and Dan walked a distance of about a mile and a half to the nearest Rest Centre which was Cloberhill School in Great Western Road. We were given a welcome cup of tea and some biscuits. Dan took some kind of fit here and we thought it was the end of him after all he had gone through but he took a huge drink of water when he recovered a bit and we assumed that it was just a drink he needed. There were so many human beings to attend to that a dog was not top priority (he was to me).

The following day, having had no sleep, we tried to salvage what we could take away from our house, especially clothing, but found that someone had been there before us and helped themselves to some of our things, silly things such as my music case filled with sheet music. It was difficult to know what exactly had been taken as the place was in such a mess. We did not own any things of great value – just personal items but our attitude was that so many lives had been lost and others ruined that it did not seem to matter. It was a case of getting on with things as best you could as the authorities were so over-run they were no help at all.

We lived at the bus terminus and while we were in the remains of our house a bus appeared believe it or not through all the debris and who stepped off but my grandma from Torrance. Only a suffragette would have attempted that journey! She took one look at the state of things and assured that we were all alive got the same bus back into town and then her Torrance bus- no telephones or mobile phones so it was the only way she could find out if we had survived, she was a tough cookie.

The following night, 14th March, we had another raid which was also scary and we were at a friend's house in Maryhill, hoping to get away from the Clyde which was an attraction for bombers but nothing fell on Scotstounhill that night and we got a few at Maryhill which proved to us that we just stay put from then on

The most poignant memory of the 13th March was the direct hit of the First Aid Centre at Bankhead School, Knightswood. A land mine fell on it doing terrible damage. It was the pivotal centre for the area and lots of doctors, nurses and firemen were lost but the saddest maybe were the young lads of 15 or 16 years who volunteered as messengers between the various centres in the area. They were all killed , I'm not certain how many but quite a few . Boys of this age think that they are immortal and no doubt felt quite important doing this job. Health and safety were unheard of then! When Bankhead School was rebuilt there was a plaque put up for all who were killed.

My cousin Annie had her wedding planned for the end of March but she cancelled the Hotel arrangements and had a quiet reception in her parent's house in Dumbarton Road which was not damaged. Annie and her fiancé Andrew, who worked with the Housing Department of the then Glasgow Corporation had been allocated a new house in Glencoe Street, Anniesland ready to go into after they were married, as one did in those days – had to be married!!!

Our family got the use of it for the two weeks prior to their marriage, no furniture or carpets, just beds on the floor and a few cooking utensils. We were lovely and warm though as it had the new back to back range in the kitchen and living room. Annie said that her house had been taken over by squatters before she had even lived in it.

Anniesland Station was nearby so I travelled from there to my office in Hope Street. It did not feel the same as travelling from Scotstounhill as we knew most people who travelled regularly and at Anniesland I knew no-one and thought that they were a bit 'snooty' which was probably only in my mind but I did miss the usual company. Mr Sweet my boss in the office must have felt sorry for me as he arranged for me to have my lunch at Miss Buick's restaurant in West George Street for as long as it took to get normality again which was quite some time. I certainly enjoyed eating out as this was a new experience to me. It felt a bit strange at first but I soon became more confident in ordering my food and most days had the main course and trifle and ice cream to follow which I loved as rations did not run to this at home. Tea and cake followed – a great life.

Once again unfortunately I lost my close chums as they spread out all over the place till our houses were repaired. Margaret ended up in Strathaven for the nine months or so we were homeless.

At fifteen years of age friends are an important part of your life sharing all sorts of secrets but it was a great day when we were re-united again.

After living at Anniesland we moved in with friends of my parents who lived in Dumbarton Road near Kingsway. They were Tommy and Jeanie Furzer and lived in the ground floor of a three storey tenement. My parents and I shared a large front room and Alastair stayed with Aunt Mary across the road sharing a room with Uncle Alec my mother's brother. This continued until our house was habitable again. Tommy and Jeannie were a lovely couple and made us very welcome – Dan included.

Tommy Furzer was a signalman in the London & Midland Scottish Railway and worked in a signal box at Scotstoun. He was quite a character and a comedian at times especially when he had a few drinks, a bit too much often but never aggressive with it. He lost his false teeth down the loo when he was sick once and Jeannie gave him a swearing calling him all things. To me it was funny but his wife had to fish them out of the loo as he was not capable so she was far from impressed. All things considered though they were a happy couple. We played card games a lot while we lived at Dumbarton Road and those games continued with my parents every Friday night when we returned to our own house. Newmarket seemed to be a favourite and they played for a halfpenny a time, big time indeed!

Soon after we arrived at the Furzer's house dad was made redundant with a printing firm in Hillington who made greetings cards for all occasions. We had a large case full of cards so never needed to buy any for years. His work was not considered essential to the war effort and the firm of J&G Ponton was taken over by a munitions factory. He had been employed at this factory for a number of years and enjoyed the work so he was upset about it but soon got another job which made paper bags and envelopes (not as artistic as the other job)

Just to add to the horrible year of 1941 I took ill in June with an ovarian cyst and was sent to the Western Infirmary for tests – via tramcar and in lots of pain. There I saw a gynaecologist by the name of Dr McKay Hart who diagnosed a cyst on the ovary and would require an operation. He was a young doctor starting out in his career and to further his knowledge he said he would like to perform the operation himself but the only way to guarantee this was to put me in a private nursing home at no charge. The nursing home was in

Burnbank Gardens, near George's cross so I spent three weeks there in luxury. A long time by to-day's standards, a week of that time was spent in bed completely!

Dr Hart became an eminent gynaecologist at the Western Infirmary – very well respected and sought after so I hope I managed to further his career. He attended Douglas's birth ten years later but I doubt if he really remembered me

Mum was a staunch member of the Labour Part and a socialist all her life so 'Nursing Homes' were not in her vocabulary. However I'm sure that on this occasion she was pleased with the attention I got from an up and coming doctor.

I made a good recovery from the operation minus half an ovary and of course the cyst which I believe was kept in a jar for future doctors to peruse. It was the size of a grapefruit and had hair and bones (yuk) . According to the experts it could have been a twin of mine that had not developed but who knows. I may have had the sister I always wanted (wonder if it is still in a jar at the Western!) My time in the nursing home was interesting apart from the operation. Being young myself the domestics and nurses came to me with all their stories of their love lives. The telephone box opposite the nursing home was used by the staff to phone boyfriends and they also met them there as I saw from my window and I would give them a wave. Sounds a bit tame and daft nowadays but my only other entertainment was reading and eating. Thus ends the story of my operation and the twin I may have had.

Before Christmas of that year we moved back in to our repaired house minus glass in windows as there was a shortage of glass like many other things so we had a waterproof white canvas sort of stuff which let in the light but we could not see out which was a bit weird but we were getting used to weird happenings by this time. The house was probably colder because of the lack of glass but I can't remember if I felt the cold just glad to be back in our home again and looking forward to meeting my chums again.

A 'Grant' was given by the government for essentials to bombed households for furniture, dishes and all the other requirements for a home. My room had a new three piece suite which was called Utility furniture which as the name suggests was very basic but I was delighted as it was the first new furniture I had owned. We had managed to save some of our living room furniture as it was at the front of the house and was Victorian stuff which had been passed down through the family so it withstood the bombing quite well although was pitted with glass from the windows when the bomb fell. The War Damage Commission requested a list of all that we had lost in the bombing and a friend of mum's who had a stamp shop in West Nile Street (William Ferris) did the valuating and advised us to overestimate as we were bound to forget some items as did happen. Our pictures were described as 'etchings' thus getting more money. A bit sneaky really but this was quite common and we found later that we had forgotten some items. A funny story here as a friend of mine, Nan Sutherland,
who survived the blitz in Clydebank said that the assessors in Clydebank were amazed at how many people owned pianos! No-one could prove anything and pianos were worth a fair bit of money so if you claimed for a piano you were 'quids

in'. We actually owned a piano which was mine and it was pitted with glass but we never claimed. My brother took it off to New Zealand where he went with his family for six months before coming home disillusioned minus piano. I was miffed but that is another story which does happen in families.

Isaac Shields a family friend had some source of getting large stone jars of jam and fruit and other scarce items of food (probably black market). We never asked questions as rationing was severe and we were always glad to see him. Any kind of fruit tinned or otherwise was not available so it was a real treat. He was a bit of a blether when he came but we put up with that.

Thanks to the ingenuity of mum we never went hungry, looking back now as an adult, women at home did an amazing job queuing for food, cooking with practically nothing. Potatoes and bread always seemed to be available, the bread being unrefined thus a dark colour but we got used to it and it had added vitamins so quite good for us. There were certainly not many fat people around and the health of the nation was not bad considering. Obese was not in the vocabulary.

Just as we were settling down nicely in our newly decorated house and my lovely room my gran came to stay with us sharing my room as there was no alternative. The bright spark that we had known developed dementia and got very confused. The poor wee Torrance grocer, who had known her for many years, was at his wits end with her denying that she had received her rations for the week. She probably ate them all on the day that she bought them for she had a good appetite. It was obvious that something had to be done. Gran and I got on well together and I have many pleasant memories of days out and evenings at the cinema in Kirkintilloch but sharing my room and speaking to her long dead friends and relations into the night put a strain on our relationship especially when I was also accused of wearing her clothes! We had to make the best of things but at my young age it was far from easy. Mum found it difficult also as she lifted items from Woolworths and never paid for them far less give coupons. We had quite a stock of ladies' hankies if I remember right. Another item she brought home was fish and it was often hidden under her mattress causing a stink. She was sometimes brought home in the early hours by the police because she lost her way but never accused of stealing which was a relief.

She had a strong heart and proved it by walking around Kelvingrove Park which was one of her old haunts, then called The West End Park. Sometimes she was soaked through but never had as much as a sniffle. She was used to long walks with Bob in and around Torrance so there was no way of keeping her in at Danes Drive. It was always amazing how she mostly found her way home from those long walks. Gran stayed with us for two years when she had finally to be admitted to the Southern General Hospital where she seemed remarkably happy thinking that this was her new house and the visitors her friends.

Visiting was done mainly by foot via the Whiteinch Ferry which on a windy day was blown up the Clyde but somehow managed to reach Govan safely.. The round trip took a few hours but we spread out the visiting between the family but I know that mum did most of the visiting. Gran did not recognise most of us by that time. A sad end to someone who had a colourful life and never suffered fools gladly.

Dan was in 'doggie heaven' by this time so one day on the spur of the moment (as I often do) I bought a tiny dog from Wilsons Zoo in Oswald Street. The family were surprised when I walked in with this dog hardly larger than my hand. Fortunately mum took a liking to him and we named him Larry but he was an odd looking wee dog. He disappeared when he was about five years on Douglas's first birthday and was never seen again but dad dug up some bones from the compost heap a number of years later and was convinced they were Larry's . He had not been very well and some dogs go and look for a place to die but we'll never know.

I come now to what could only have
been dad's 'male menopause'. He developed a kind of friendship with the daughter-in-law of the Furzers. Her name was Chrissie and George, her husband, was working during the week in Workington, Cumbria. Chrissie was a rather helpless sort of woman (mum would call her 'useless'), and was very dependant of a man about the house to lean on. Dad in my mind was the fall guy here and visited her frequently when he finished work to help her with her two young boys. Being my dad I find it hard to believe he was 'stud' material and he was a generation older than her but she was the clinging vine type so maybe this attracted him as my mum certainly was not. Dad would have liked a stay at home wife with his slippers heating at the fire but instead of that he got someone who was more interested in Labour Party meetings

and the like. I must add here that she also did a good job of looking after her family and we never suffered.

Mum and I discussed his 'affair' and I know she was quite hurt and upset. She had a badly broken leg at the time sustained in Arran and with her leg in plaster and crutches she was looking after my dad's sister who lived in Townhead and was very ill so it meant a bus journey each day to attend to her. Dad could have hardly chosen a worse time to be 'helping' other people. As you can imagine there was a lot of talking and arguing between them but it finally sorted itself out when Chrissie joined her husband in Workington. Mum spoke to a solicitor but nothing came of it and as she said to me "why should I walk out and leave everything I've built up", which was true.

Their friendship with the senior Furzers remained and they still had their card games on a Friday night. Only once did I talk to my dad about his 'fling' and told him in no uncertain way if he did not change his ways I would have nothing more to say to him and he would no longer see Douglas. This had some effect on him.

An amusing incident happened about this time in our house. A knock at the door led to an elderly man and woman entering our house, the woman obviously ill and asking if she could sit down. Mum realised she was fairly ill as a matter of fact she was dying so she made her comfortable. Mum was very capable at such times so they came to the right house but I made myself scarce. The man who was her brother and was taking her to the bus stop and was very nervous of the whole thing. The long and short of it was that she died and a coffin appeared in our house to take her away. Alastair had been sleeping upstairs and came to see what all the commotion was about as they were edging the coffin out the front door. I will never forget the expression on his face as he tried to wake himself up. It took him some time to gather himself together and realise that it was none of the family then off he went to bed again – typical Alastair. The brother appeared a few weeks later with some money for us but mum refused it saying she would be a poor specimen if she took payment for such a thing and advised him to give it to charity. He came from a large house in Anniesland Road and probably thought we would grab the money being poor council tenants.Mum went throught all this with a broken leg, plaster and crutches holding the patients hand till she died the woman's brother going back to Anniesland Road for reinforcements.

Margaret Hutchison (Kelly) lived across the road in Danes Drive and we were both keen on ballroom dancing and we frequented the Albert Ballroom in Bath Street (near the King's Theatre). The Albert was known to be more 'sedate' than some of the other venues in Glasgow and also it was on the bus route with a bus stop at the door. Dance halls such as the Locarno in Sauchiehall Street were popular with the American forces and attracted a certain clientele who followed the Americans around because of the money they had and also tights which were not on sale in Britain. Lots of GI Brides and babies after the war! My opinion of the Americans was that they were very overpowering and sure of themselves, probably because they were away from home. We stuck mainly to the Albert although occasionally branched out elsewhere.

Our other dancing friend was Netta Queen but she met a boy
who seemed very nice but within the year she was pregnant
(at eighteen years). She was a quiet girl,with a smashing
looking brother, and Margaret and I were quite taken aback
but she married the guy and things did not go well ending
badly. She did have a lovely wee girl and an understanding
mother. Eventually she married again and this time it all went
well but her dancing days were not so frequent.

Margaret and I met George and Archie in 1942 at the Albert
although George insists he first saw me at the Woodend in
Chamberlain Road – I don't remember this so he could not
have made an impression!

Archie was a joiner (a very good one) and he had only one
useful eye due to an accident in childhood. They were
making a gate at Foxbar Drive where George lived and they
invited us to come and watch them (how romantic is that?)
After a bit of discussion between us Margaret and I decided
to cycle to Foxbar and see this gate but we pussyfooted
around before having the nerve to stop at number 46.
Margaret was keen on Archie thinking that he resembled
Sean Connery and that was enough for
her.George was already going out with a girl called Jeannie
but Ithink the fact that she lived at the other side of Glasgow
and I just lived a short distance away settled it for him. He
told me later that he did not like her legs when she went
upstairs in the tram in front of him. Made me conscious of
my legs when I preceded him upstairs!

I received a letter from George about two or three weeks
after the garden gate rendezvous in three colours of ink,
technicolour he called it, which I have kept all those years.

It's a piece of history now as few letters must be written what with email, text and all the other stuff around in this era A handwritten letter delivered through the post is bound to be more romantic.
 (showing my age here)..To get back to this great invitation to see him again my response was that I was washing my hair that night. He must have admired my imagination! He had another try a few weeks later wondering if I had washed my hair and if I would go to the cinema with him. Fed up playing hard to get I agreed to meet him. Jeannie was off the scene by now so that was the start of the next sixty odd years. Margaret and I met George and Archie often in the Albert inside thus paying our own way which left us free to dance with others – not daft. George and Archie were serving appreticeships so had very little money. My bus fare was paid going home but sometimes I had a bus pass whuch must have made his day!

George and Archie were cousins and very close seeing each other often. Archie's mother was a single parent and had a large ground floor flat in John Street in the centre of Glasgow . She was not always in the best of health but she took in boarders for a living as she had always been in service since leaving school so had a bit of experience. She was a good plain cook. She did neglect herself and I remember her ulcers on her legs and being unable to walk far but she worked hard to keep Archie. He spent a lot of time at Foxbar Drive which was almost his second home and although Sarah was his aunt he called her 'mum'. He also went week-ends to Bathgate where he stayed with another couple calling them mum and dad also, they were very good to Archie and he liked going there. It could be said that he had not a stable life but Archie grew into a great guy nevertheless which maybe proves something.

Margaret was a bit jealous of the friendship between George and Archie – with Margaret it was all or nothing and she had to be the king pin so she pretty well monopolised Archie. In all honesty Archie was besotted with Margaret so I don't suppose he was complaining. Was room for both if she had allowed it and he had stood up to her which he was too good natured to do (too much in love also).

We did see quite a bit of them but George rarely saw Archie on his own which was a pity. He died suddenly when he was only 56 years of a stroke. George and I saw him in hospital and it was very sad to see a fine looking tanned man unable to speak and hardly able to move. He worked outside a lot so that's what made him look so well. Margaret once again did not play fair with George at this time as it was her mother who phoned us to say that Archie was ill and she felt that Margaret was not going to tell him. Margaret was surprised when George and I turned up at the hospital but Archie looked pleased to see George so that was all that mattered. He died the following day and it
was so sad to think that such a lovely man had died so young. I've drifted away from my story somewhat but thought that Archie was well worth a mention.

Margaret lived till her late 70's and had an active life (Bingo etc.) She collapsed in Bishopbriggs town centre after a night out beside a police car which would have pleased her no end and the final exit executed well!!

Returning to our younger days 1943-4 Margaret and I decided we would have to earn more cash to help finance our hectic nights at the Albert. Frank Leach, a friend of my parents owned a newsagents shop in Netherton, Anniesland and required someone to help with the book-keeping side of the business so Margaret, being fully experienced with White Horse Whisky offices and myself being able to add up felt that this was a doddle on a Sunday morning apart from getting out of bed on time.We hauled out our bicycles and began our wee job sorting out the books which were a bit of a mess. We got them into some sort of order between us and enjoyed the money but after about a year doing this Margaret was unable to come one Sunday so I went on my own.

Frank and I chatted away a bit before I started on the books but to my complete amazement I realized he was trying it on a bit so I made for the door quickly and literally got on my bike – no wages.This was a man of my dad's generation whom I had known all my life and I really could not believe it. Mum and I used to visit him at a holiday hut in Balmore occasionally. He was overweight and rather ugly but always seemed a nice enough man so maybe he had a brainstorm or something.

I never told my parents the reason for leaving Frank's shop as I was slightly embarrassed so she thought we just got fed up. My dad would have punched him probably. Margaret and I had a good giggle after but that was the end of our wee job. It made me wary of older men for a while even the ones I knew. Sexual harassment was not in vogue those d ays and we never had a nervous breakdown about it but

Margaret and I had a few laughs and got on with life adding it to our experiences.

George was called up for the Royal Corp of Signals in December 1944 and it surprised and upset us as we always thought that he was in what was called a reserved occupation serving his time with the Albion Motors but no arguments he had to report to a training camp at Fort George, Inverness-shire, freezing cold mid-winter. The course was 8 weeks duration and he hated every minute of it as the whole idea was to toughen them up and it did. No mummy in those places to spoil you!

After the initial training he was posted to Huddersfield in the midlands and things were easier there although still tough. He was in Huddersfield during the summer months so I spent a week of my holidays with him, not literally as he had to live in at barracks so I had 'digs' with an elderly lady who did not go out a lot, probably had arthritis or something, so I shopped for her most days and we seemed to live on salads. It meant that I got to know the area quite well although I was on my own as I only saw George in the evenings and we usually went to the cinema as there was not much else to do. The week soon went in and I had to return on the busy smokey trains, standing a large part of the way. When the train came in to Huddersfield station George spotted a seat beside a girl so he handed his hat in for her to put it on the empty seat next her. I struggled in with my case and sat down. George can remember the look on her face when she realised it was not a fella that was taking the seat I cannot say that I was aware of this- probably a bit naive'

When I changed trains at Crewe or somewhere I had to sit on my case in the corridor along with a bunch of servicemen. They kept me supplied with chocolate which was rationed to us civilians I was eighteen years and felt mature which I'm sure I was as war time made you grow up quickly and I had been working for nearly four years. On arrival at Central Station me and my case had to haul ourselves to the nearest bus stop. No cars or parents to pick us up. My parents had never heard from me for a week as we had no telephone – such a vast difference to-day where there seems to be constant contact. Will be interesting to know how they turn out as adults but I will not be around to find out but generations seem to sort themselves out.

After several months in Huddersfield George was posted to Scarborough for further training which seemed to please him as there were many dance halls there being a seaside resort. Getting his own back no doubt as I still continued at the Albert while he was away.

In December 1945 he was drafted out to Port Said in Egypt which seemed a long way away. He sailed and was very seasick which put him off long sails for life. We wrote to each other every day and I wonder now what we got to say. Sometimes the letters piled up and I would get 5 or 6 at a time so had to sort them out in order or I would not know what he was talking about. Our postman was a gem and he looked for me each morning when I was going for the train. I was probably keeping him in a job!

In December 1946 he got leave for a whole month then back to Port Said for another 365 letters. For some reason he was

not as sick this time but the boats were very packed and not very comfortable sleeping in hammocks As for myself I had another very lonely year to look forward to and it took some time to settle down again after the month leave but
that was the consequence of war.

Margaret and I continued dancing at the Albert the only difference being that she still had Archie but there was a group we knew well so I was not entirely alone but of course not the same without George. They were purely dancing partners and
nothing more some of them being boring but good dancers. George had his special partners also so that was how it went. Out of the blue an RAF guy who was on two weeks embarkation leave before being posted abroad asked me if I would go to the cinema with him. He knew George and said he would understand if I refused his invite which I did. We were a mannerly lot in those days and he stressed it would only be for two
weeks.Margaret thought I was mad not to enjoy a bit of life as she put it. He managed to get on the same bus as me occasionally as he lived in Lincoln Avenue but that was as far a
s it went apart from the dancing He asked me to write to him abroad but one letter a day to George was more than I could cope with. The last time I saw him before he went abroad he gave me his address in the off chance that I would split from George. Nice to think I had someone to fall back on................There was an urgen
cy during war years and friendships moved along quicker probably because we never lnew what tomorrow would bring.

105

When we lived with the Furzers in Dumbarton Road I became friendly with Winnie McAdam (Hillis) who lived across the road and below my Aunt Mary in a tenement building. By a strange set of circumstances Winnie's mother and my mother attended the same school in the Gorbals when they were kids. They were also keen members of the Co-op Guild in Kingsway. Winnie was engaged to Don Hillis who lived in Clydebank and was a trumpeter in the Clydebank Burgh Band which had a high status in those days. Many of his family were also in the band and they were well known in Clydebank as they had cousins everywhere coming from a large family.

Don worked in the shipyards but travelled around with the band in his spare time but did not always include Winnie so we attended some of the performances as it was the only way they saw each other. Winnie and I were avid cinema goers so between that and visiting her many cousins and Aunts we kept occupied.

Winnie and Don along with daughter Margaret then aged two years decided to emigrate to Canada which was surprising as Winnie was very much a 'home girl' and was in close touch with her many relations and she also could not stand watching 'goodbyes' in stations usually ending up crying along with them.. Don was also leaving a large close family but he had got a job in Canada so was determined to give it a try. It was somewhat of a wrench when they left and I missed Winnie lots but she returned home on occasions for visits until after her mum and dad died then her visits became less.

She died from throat cancer (smoker) around 2005 and I have no information what happened to Don.

Back to the mid forties when I joined a Clydebank Dramatic Club who rehearsed in the Town Hall which surprisingly survived the Blitz almost intact although the area around was a bit knocked about. We had a great producer who managed to get the best out of us being full of enthusiasm himself. Rehearsals were great fun, we did some one act plays and also four act ones which took some memorising Our annual show was held in the Town Hall which I have been to recently with Lesley and it seems almost in a time warp looking similar as it was in the forties which gave me a feeling of De ja Vu (good French eh?) When George returned to civilian life in 1947 I drifted away from the Dramatic Club having other things on my mind probably.

About this time I left the office in Hope Street to go to the wages department in Babcock & Wilcox in Renfrew. Alastair and my Uncle Alex both worked there and praised it highly but the wages office was immense and did not appeal to me having worked in a smaller environment and being much closer to all that was going on. I only did one part of the wage sheet then it was passed on to another section which was really boring. The girl helping me to settle in was a staunch Salvation Army member who did not believe in doing very much except attend their meetings which was a bit of a conversation stopper. The canteen where we all ate was enormous also although the food was quite nice but soon got fed up with that too.

To add to all this 'trauma' we were having the worst winter for years with snow up to our knees, trams off and having to walk to the Renfrew Ferry, about a mile or so and another walk at Yoker of about the same, all in deep snow and freezing cold. This lasted for three months. We started work at 8.30am and finished at 5.30pm plus two nights overtime till 9pm. After eight weeks of this I had enough and got a job with a flooring firm in South Street, Whiteinch.

I now cycled to my new firm which only took me about ten minutes which was sheer joy after the journey to Renfrew and I did not have to depend on transport. Even if I did not have my bike one of the two directors of the firm gave Rena, the other female and myself a run home. They were great bosses, a real family business. Some fifty workmen were employed in J.G.Robertson who laid flooring on many of the large liners on the Clyde such as the Queen Mary and Queen Elizabeth. Being a small firm suited me fine and I loved my work which consisted of preparing the wages for the workmen from their worksheets right through to making up the wages with the Cashier on a Friday which was much more interesting than only doing the one part of them as in Babcocks. We had a close rapport with the workmen and had many a good laugh at their exploits. Occasionally Rena and I were taken to one of the super liners on the Clyde to see the finished object and we loved that as the furnishings on the liners were fabulous.

A year after I started at Whiteinch the firm moved to Whitecrook Street in, Clydebank beside the canal. The offices were larger with lots more storage place for flooring and although it was further to cycle I enjoyed working in

Clydebank. When George and I got married in 1949 we were given a present of flooring in the house at Foxbar Drive which was top quality as you can imagine. I left when Douglas appeared.

Mum was a member or I should say a Founder member of the Kingsway Co-operative Women's Guild which had meetings locally every week. She was renowned for her hard work and devotion to the Labour Party and the Co-operative movement, most of her spare time being spent at one meeting or another. She thrived on it and I am convinced that in future generations she would have been successful as a politician. Dad did not support her in this and resented the time she spent in her pursuits so to keep the peace she back pedalled a bit. It certainly did not affect her responsibilities in the home as she was always there with meals etc. so I don't know what his problem was. There was friction in the house and talks of a split at one time but if she had followed her heart she would have had no financial backing so that was not on the cards. Alastair and I were independent by this time so we were spreading our wings a bit. That was just how things were in those days – the woman was expected to be at the sink. I was aware of the fact that in Danes Drive where we lived most mothers were at home and our mum seemed to be different but that's the way it was and all credit to her. Before her death in 1973 she expressed a wish for a private funeral with no Labour Party or Co-operative members to attend This surprised me greatly and I never found out the reason for her change of heart but we did as she wished. Many of her friends were upset about this but nothing could be done about it so we had a family only funeral. Her friends formed a guard of honour at her house when the funeral left so I wonder what she would have thought about that..

To get back to the Guild which met once a week in whatever locations were available during the blackout days of the war.Those women have to be admired for their stoicism with usually a full membership each week often in extreme conditions but never complaining and enjoying the company as many had sons or other relatives serving abroad, some missing in action , some killed and some in prisoner of war camps not having seen them for many years. The Guild was obviously a life line and helped them through very difficult times. I knew all of them and for the remainder of their lives were a very strong breed of women not seen to-day in our soft society. (no reference to my family here!)

Mum formed a Dramatic Club in the Guild which proved very successful and her aim was to try and lift the spirits of her fellow members which it did as they were an enthusiastic bunch. It has to be remembered that there was no television then so making your own entertainment was the thing to do and it kept them sane being occupied. They often met for rehearsals in each others houses which kept the cost of hiring a hall to a minimum. Aunt Mary (mum's sister) was a lovely singer so she formed a choir which was also popular, both running for many years.

The annual concert was held in the Partick Burgh Halls and turned out to be a fairly big event. I played the piano accompaniment to the songs in the choir so it was a family affair. Winnie was a Highland Dancer so she was also cajoled into doing her bit. Other people added to the programme so it was a varied performance. Maybe would not go down so well in 2010 but in the 1940's, with many theatres closed we sold most of the tickets.

The war in Europe ended in 1945 (April if I remember right) and the war in the Far East went on until August 1945. A lot has been said about the end of the war but to me personally it was absolute relief and a time of my life I have no wish to repeat. There were good times and very bad times with all the shortages of clothes etc. but most of all was the fear of being killed so living without that was best of all. Shortages remained for many years and we had ten years or so of meagre living with things improving slowly but at least we had survived when many did not.

Celebrations for V.E.day were great fun perhaps heightened by the knowledge that we were no longer in danger and that life would improve slowly. Winnie, Don and Don's brother Jim who was home on leave at the time and myself of course, walked from Scotstoun to Clydebank enjoying one big party, streets packed but no violence everyone so happy and letting their hair down without the aid of booze which was in short supply. Food was also not plentiful but we did not miss it , I think we had fish suppers on the way home. It was a memorable episode in our lives but tame by to-day's standards I suppose. Nevertheless we were happy beyond comprehension and I now knew that George would not be involved in any fighting with an enemy.

Clydebank was still very much in recovery, some families back in their homes or re-built homes and enjoying the moment but not forgetting the many families who lost relations and sometimes whole families wiped out, grandparents down to babies, uncles and aunts etc. As I have grown older I feel that wars are rather glorified by some sections, all the pomp on armistice day and the like can never make up for the fact that a town such as Clydebank was almost wiped out in a matter of hours killing thousands of people and hideously injuring others – nothing glorious or heroic about that.

Mum's feelings were that my generation had lost their important teen years because of the war but I never thought about it like that as I never knew anything else and we were all in the same boat and enjoying ourselves as teenagers do but in a different way because of the shortages of clothes, make up etc. which were paramount to us, to such an extent that when Boots got their supply of make up there was a mad dash and a queue to stand in to get one lipstick maybe. It was comparable
 to winning the Lottery!.

Education wise I will never know how well or otherwise I would have progressed at school which is maybe just as well as I've always had the war to blame but in
 the 1970's I sat an exam of 'O' Grade level to get in to Clydebank College to brush up on my secretarial skills and passed that so I suppose that is better than nothing.

Ration books were finally abolished in 1952. I had become expert in the use of dried egg and even preferred it when real shell eggs became available again as it was so easy to bake with and knew exactly the quantities so it took some time to get accustomed to using the real hen eggs. I believe powdered egg is still available in some shops but why anyone would use it beats me.

I realise now how much stress and strain our parents must have had seeing their teenagers going out in the blackout with the dangers of air raids added to it also no means of communication via telephone to let tham know you were safe. The one restriction I had put on me was that I had to get the last bus home which was at 10.45pm, the terminus being at our door almost. I missed it once and mum was waiting for me behind the door about 11.30pm and delivered a hefty clout. I was sixteen at the time and thought that she was a bit hard on me but know now that she must have been very worried not knowing where I was. I never missed the bus again!.

Mum was well known for carrying a large hatpin behind her coat lapel in case of the necessity to use it if she was accosted which I don't think she ever was but believe me she would have used it.

During the latter part of the war years mum was going through the menopause and had a few problems to add to the stresses of keeping food on the table for the family. One problem was an overactive thyroid gland which was treated (unsuccessfully I think) with iodine drops. She was also plagued by headaches which was probably migraine from the sound of it. She liked to think that she could treat herself with paracetamol etc. but she did visit her G.P. once or twice and you may find it hard to believe now but he suggested cigarette smoking as it would calm her nerves. Smoking was common in those days before the dangers were discovered. I saw her with the odd cigarette but it was not financially possible to continue so perhaps that was for the best.

George was demobbed in 1947 and we were pleased to get back to a more normal life again as both of us had no doubts about continuing our lives as before having both matured in those three years.

George returned to the Albion Motors, his apptrenticeship completed so he was now earning more money.

We bought a tandem from some friends, a Selmar which was top of the range but quite heavy as bikes were then. It took a bit of getting used to as I was used to a single bike and it seemed peculiar sitting at the back not steering. I soon got the hang of it and was often accused of -not pedalling hard enough but I had more time to admire the scenery around me.

We cycled on Sundays, weather permitting, going to Helensburgh, Gareloch and sometimes Largs. I was dropped off at home, had a bath then went to Foxbar where there was a lovely meal waiting for us prepared y Granny Barr who was a good plain cook having been in 'service' in her younger days. Very often she cooked rabbit which was not on the ration having been soaked in a bowl of salted water overnight which made it tender. Seeing it lying in the bowl reminded me of what an abortion must look like but by the time it was cooked for several hours with plenty veggies it tasted great. A bit stronger than chicken.

After the meal we attempted the Sunday Post crossword (trying not to get too excited!). Jessie and Rennie were also there and Jessie got most of the clues. We all sat round an open fire with Flash the alsation dog spread in front of it getting all the heat but we rested our legs (mine usually tired) on top of him and he never batted an eyelid – a lovely dog.

We were keen cinema goers and went about twice a week and twice to the Albert, money permitting. We were just so pleased to be able to pick our lives up again after the long break. When money was short George came to my house and mum allowed us to use my room – being very broad minded. I always got something nice for his supper and actually enjoyed making it for him (happy days).

George took an interest in Partick Thistle at Firhill and accompanied my dad some Saturdays becoming a keen supporter eventually. Rennie being a footballer himself and playing for the R.A.F. team joined forces with them at a later date. Sheila also went with them and was lifted over the turnstyle till she was well over fifteen years (being a petite sort of person). Her interest in sport must have been evident even then.

George and I got engaged on my birthday in November 1948 and planned to marry the following year. We were married on 23rd September 1949 in St David's Church, Knightswood and held the reception in the Grand Hotel at Charing Cross which was a lovely hotel but is no longer there because of the M8 motorway which was the cause of many nice buildings being demolished.

Our honeymoon was spent in Scarborough where George had done some of his army training so he was quite impressed with the place. It may seem pretty tame now but the war had only been over for four years so long distance travel was not an option for us even if we had been able to fund it.

We stayed at Foxbar Drive for the first ten years of our married life with George's mother – she had two rooms upstairs and we had two rooms downstairs plus kitchen, not an ideal arrangement but houses were very hard to get in those post war days so this seemed a good option. It worked out most of the time but there were moments when tempers were stretched as you can imagine especially when I gave up work when the children arrived. She was very much family orientated and she would have liked to have had more input in Douglas and Sheila's lives but I was young and had my own ideas. Her intentions were well meant but living so close I did not see things that way and fought against it. George's sister Jessie lived in Partick so she spent a lot of time looking after Ian as Jessie had returned to work and when Jessie and family moved to Corby where Rennie had got a job she spent some time down there which gave us the house to ourselves. Granny Sarah was a genuine person and her and her sister Mary had a very hard life as children as they were boarded out when they were very young to a farm in the north of Scotland. We do not know what happened to their parents, but they were not treated well in the farm they were in so had a hard life. This probably accounted for the need of a family in her later years.

As Douglas and Sheila grew older, when they were eight and four, we were in need of more room so we bought our first house in Windyedge Crescent, Jordanhill. We had lots of discussion with Granny Sarah and she finally accepted the fact that we had to move.It so happened that Jessie and Rennie had moved from Corby to Johnstone as Rennie missed watching Partick Thistle (or so he said). They hated Johnstone so decided to move in with Granny Sarah when we left which suited Granny fine as Jessie was working so she looked after the children during the day. Everybody happy!

Windyedge Crescent was a very close community where everyone knew your movements which took a bit of getting used to. Lesley was born there in 1963 at 9am and the whole street knew as soon as I did almost. When she was six months old we moved to Eastcote Avanue, a bigger more substantial house arriving with three children and a mad poodle (Bramble). An older couple lived next door so they must have wondered what had hit them as two elder maiden ladies had been there before us. The garden was walled so it was different to Windyedge Crescent which felt a bit funny at first

As a matter of interest the house in Windyedge cost us £2400 in 1959 and the house in Eastcote Avenue cost £3400 on 1964. It's worth a bit more now !!!.

My story about finishes here as we still live at Eastcote Avenue a mere 48 years, dad aged 88 years and myself 86 years. We now appreciate the help of both Sheila and Lesley for being able to remain here.

It seems my story is not finished as Sheila and Lesley think I should continue it I'm sure they just want to keep me occupied. Maybe something to be said for carrying on with my blethers as I still do not go out a lot apart from shopping and I take the car which is a godsend. Doctor thinks I may have Spinal Stenosis so at least got a name for it but can't come up with a cure so as the old saying goes 'what can't be cured must be endured'

. I suppose the best place to start again is when George and I got married.

Our first year of marriage living in the house of George's widowed mother, Sarah, was a case of getting used to married life and also a mother-in-law who was not the type to fade into the background. She rather liked the idea of company. It being a council rented house we took over paying all bills but she was officially the Queen Bee of the house as her name was on the rental agreement as she reminded us occasionally when she thought it necessary. George also gave her one pound per week as a wee pressie which I suppose could be the equivalent of about ten pounds to-day or more so she was well looked after financially. (no problems there!)

It was common practice to live with family in 1949 as housing was scarce. I had a friend, Nancy McKinnon who also was in the same situation and lived nearby in Knightswood with her mother-in-law so we griped to each other when things got out of hand.

I returned to work with JG Robertson in Clydebank which was good as

it earned us money and I also liked my work and the company, better than being at home all day as some women did when they married. I was home in time to make a meal but too often Sarah had made something for us which, being young and newly married, I resented (could do with her now). Sarah had to be held at arms length or she would have taken over our lives. The arrangement was that Sarah had two rooms upstairs with bathroom and we had two rooms downstairs with kitchenette. A large cupboard on the landing upstairs acted as a cooking area for Sarah. This usually worked alright except when it did not and she appeared downstairs to our cooker. Health and Safety would have a nervous breakdown today knowing that a cooker was in a cupboard but no emergencies happened.

I wanted to do my own thing completely but Sarah was not good at standing back. The message got through to her eventually and she backed off a bit but she was not easy to ignore.

My mum was so different from Sarah and we had almost to make an appointment if we wanted child minding as she had a very busy life which was no problem and I was glad she had made a life for herself in her latter years. Sarah was a member of a bowling club in Bearsden which she attended occasionally. But she had few friends which I think was a throw back from her and her sisters early life when they could trust no-one. Having to live under the same roof we had to make an effort so it was not all bad.

George and I planned a trip to France on our tandem in July 1950 and we travelled by sleeper from Glasgow to London. The sleeper was shared by four people with a curtain between us and the strange thing was that we knew the other couple which was a bit of a coincidence. We then got another train to Newhaven and the ferry across to Dieppe I think. Now that we were in France it was all cycling but the weather was smashing and the roads were fairly flat. We had two panier bags on either side of the wheel at the back and this carried all our stuff. We also took a tent which was rolled up and put at my back but we soon found out that B&B was quite cheap (just five years after the war) so we posted our tent home to lighten our load. We made tea on a primus stove at lunch with some of the lovely long French bread which tasted like nothing else before usually with French cheese – gorgeous. At night we booked into a hotel and had a big feast on food we had never tasted before, not forgetting the wine. Remember rationing was still in Britain at that time. How the French managed to have such lovely food when they were an occupied country for so many years beats me.

In late 1950's I became ill with severe panic attacks and a fear of closed spaces like cinemas etc. The doctor referred me to a psychologist near C
haring Cross who, to say the least of it was decidedly odd, and probabl;y I was more grounded than her. However I had to give her a chance as I was a bit desperate which you would have to be to pour your heart out to Dr Salmon. She took me through my
 life and when it came to our house being bombed she brightened up considerably. I told her my dad and myself came through it practically unscathed but she assured me that mentally I had not and this was the cause of my illness. Then I mentioned my operation and she latched on to that. Looking back it was comical as everything I mentioned she blamed till I was as confused as her. This went on once a week for about a year till I got thoroughly fed up with her. My poor mum travelled with me on the bus every week to see this person, sometimes I got off the bus twice on the way into town but my mum was so patient and chances were that she was doing me more good than Dr Salmon. In time I decided to try and cope with the help of mum and of course George but he was working during the day and I had to have company. Mum came for me when George left for work and I stayed with her till 5pm. Going around with her to the

various activities she took part in and I cannot thank her enough for what she did at this time without complaining. George and I had several attempts at going to the cinema but often as not I refused to go in when I got to the entrance. It was really horrible and I would not wish it on my worst enemy. Sarah's help at this stage was that if I did not pull myself together George would find someone else – just what I wanted to hear but Sarah being a strong person did not fully understand so was not helpful. I think that was the reason my mum took me to her house during the day.

I became pregnant with Douglas during this time so that added to mum's work going to doctors etc. Douglas was born on 25th October 1951 at 9.30pm after a three day labour which was very unpleasant. Probably would have had a caesarean now. I was in Parkgrove Nursing Home off Woodlands Road under the care of Dr Mackay Hart who operated on me in 1941. I took some time to recover as I had many stitches and developed a fever which set me back a bit. We eventually get over most things and in time I walked out with my large Silver Cross pram hanging on to it for grim death when I felt a panic attack coming instead of taking deep breaths as we are told now.

When Douglas was able to walk I decided to make the big decision and join a Country Dancing class in the Community Centre across the road to try and fight my demons. It was difficult at first even walking out on the floor to take part in the dancing, sure I was going to faint or something worse but in time it got easier and I felt quite pleased with myself. Douglas was well behaved and sat on a seat when dancing was in progress being promised something nice to drink at the interval. He loved the music and really enjoyed himself and the attention he got from the other dancers. I made many friends at this class who helped me on the road to recovery. They did not know this as I never discussed my feelings with anyone except close family but the fact that I managed to get back out into company was a huge milestone. I first met Nancy McKinnon at this class when she came up to me one day saying what a lovely boy Douglas was. Seems he had pointed me out to her when I was on the floor dancing and said to her "That's MY mummy"!. She thought it was so sweet. (if only we could see into the future!) When I joined other classes in the evening he told people that his mummy went out dancing at night on her own so goodness knows what the people in Knightswood thought I was doing. Nancy McKinnon and myself remained close friends for many years and her husband Watson got a teaching job in Stow College where George worked. We took long walks with the prams, she eventually had two boys and at that time I had Douglas and Sheila.

We do not fully recover from those unpleasant episodes in life but manage to come to terms with them and learn to live with them and be more understanding as a result. Mum must have been delighted to see me back to near normal and able to get on with her own life which was a busy one.

When Douglas was almost two years of age we spent our first holiday in Arisaig near Mallaig which turned out to be the first of many. We had a large tent which mum and dad used in Arran in days gone by. We camped directly on the grassy beach and had what were in those days all mod cons consisting of a toilet tent, awning for cooking which stretched over the trailer used for pulling all our luggage. In the tent we had folding safari beds which were the very latest, folding chairs, very thick groundsheet and a large trunk for carrying clothes which we also used as a seat. This trunk also saw Sheila through College in Sutton Coldfield and it still takes up residence in our loft at the present time. The sands were pure white and the sea shallow so Douglas spent time with his dad spearing flat fish but they were too small to cook. It did rain at times but were absolutely dry and survived it. There were also some gorgeous sunsets which George and I enjoyed sitting in the car when Douglas was in bed. I've probably told this story before but one year, enjoying the sunset we got a lovely view of a man relieving himself in a toilet tent which was in direct line with the setting sun. Taught us a lesson on where NOT to put the toilet tent.

Sheila came along on 2nd November 1955 and was a much easier birth than Douglas. She was born in Homeland Nursing Home in Great Western Road opposite Hughenden Playing Fields where many many years later she played hockey. Homeland was run by Nuns and took care of girls who had 'fallen by the wayside' as they say. The girls did housework around the home which I suppose helped to pay for their keep. We rarely saw them in the wards for some reason. I was very happy in Homeland as the staff were very caring. Each Sunday there was a Service held in a huge hall which we could watch from above and their favourite song was The Old Wooden Cross which we joined in as there was a captive audience. The ward I was in had four patients and each of their husbands were Production Engineers at that time.which caused a few comments. I spent ten days in Homeland under the care of our GP who was Dr Cumming from the Broomhill Practice in which we are still patients to-day (2012).

We were now four in two rooms so George showed some initiative and designed a bed with a proper base which was lifted up to the wall in an alcove with two doors encasing it in day time. It was very comfortable and left the bedroom for the children. We got bunk beds from a ship that was being demolished in the Gareloch more or less for the taking away, trailer coming in handy for that. That solved our problem for the moment. Sheila seemed to prefer our bed when she could stagger in beside us so she solved her own problem. Most times she had half the bed and George and I the other half. She had stopped all this nonsense by the time she went to college!

We now had a small caravan which we parked at Rosneath Caravan Park and spent the week-ends there which gave us time on our own. Douglas enjoyed it immensely as he became friendly with Dennis Prosser whose father owned various car show rooms and of course he had a beautiful large car with all the accessories. My thoughts were that Douglas saw the car before he saw Dennis so naturally that was the friend for him. They were a bit out of our class as they owned a huge caravan and often had a nanny with them (they had three children). Mummy had a liking for the bottle also so she was always cheery when you met her. I believe that Dennis died fairly recently so that was a bit sad. Mummy became a Yoga teacher whom I met occasionally at classes but don't think she recognised me, she was alcoholic by this time but still seemed to manage the classes. Goodness knows what she taught the students

I learned to drive about 1956 and after a few lessons from George the Suez business came along which made petrol scarce so it was decided that all driving tests would be cancelled till the disagreement at Suez was settled. Learner drivers were allowed to drive without anyone sitting with them so this avoided our divorce. I think it was a good thing having to depend on yourself and other road users usually gave precedence to us – probably scared. Sheila and I often went to a nice wee quiet road and I practiced my reverse turns till I'm sure Sheila was bored out her mind but she played with her toys in the back seat (no belts) like a good wee girl and rarely complained Too
young to know the danger she was in!
George by this time was working as a lecturer in Lennox College, Dumbarton so he suggested that I could pick Douglas up at school and drive to Dumbarton on a Friday which after all was a good part of the way to Rosneath I thought he was mad and also very trusting but my driving skills were improving Granny Barr had other ideas and to say the least a bit worried but that just made me determined to prove that I could do it. I cannot explain how petrified I was the first time I did this and Douglas was warned not to talk till I got to Dumbarton. He surprised me by doing as he was told but chances were he was as petrified as me. I prayed that the traffic lights as you enter Dumbarton would be at green and they were so we arrived at the college about an hour after leaving home all in one piece. George suggested I drive the

remainder of the way to Rosneath but I will not tell you what my answer was. I felt as if I had driven to London. I sometimes did drive from Rosneath partly home but the narrow road worried me and I was really scared when a bus came into view George always assured me I had plenty room which was anything but true.

The first time I sat my test I was failed for not using the driving mirror enough so the second time I made sure that the examiner noticed I was using the mirror I could have taken him to the Helensburgh to Rosneath road and shown him a few things. When my test was about to finish that day a lorry laden with empty bottles turned the corner and unloaded the bottles around the car and all over the road. I never thought my nerves could take any more so he maybe passed me out of pity He very kindly got a brush and cleared the road for me to escape. Being able to drive meant that I did not have to travel by bus so this helped me greatly knowing that I could stop and get off any time I liked within reason so I found life a lot easier and was a lot calmer.

We took the caravan from Rosneath to our usual haunt in Arisaig for our annual two weeks holiday and in 1956 when Sheila was eight
 months old Douglas fell off a gate and broke his collar bone That year I was at Arisaig for three weeks and my mum came for one week before George was due his holidays from the Albion Motors She came by train and loved the beautiful scenery. The local doctor was not available when Douglas had his accident
as , believe it or not , he was in Inverness with his wife who

was having a baby. Those things happen in Arisaig. As mum was going home the next day and George was travelling by car up for his holidays the same day we arranged to meet in Fort William at the Belford Hospital It all worked out very well and George met us at the hospital where Douglas was seen by a top bone doctor who confirmed his collar bone was partially broken The doctors at Belford were well qualified in bone injuries due to all the mountaineers in that area. Mum continued her journey on the train back to Glasgow and we were in and out of the hospital so quickly that George managed to give her the news before the train left Fort William. Douglas had to remain fairly inactive for the remainder of the holiday.

The following year George thought it sensible to upgrade his teaching qualifications at Moray House in Edinburgh during his holiday break. It was a two week course from nine till about four pm each day. We took the caravan to North Berwick and George travelled in by train to Edinburgh each week day.This happened for a fortnight during the holidays the next year also so we got to know North Berwick very well. Granda (my dad) took a room at a boarding house nearby so we had his company during the day. Mum did her own thing at home as their marriage was not great at this time but I know she enjoyed the spell on her own doing exactly what pleased her.

There was a spooky episode happened the first year when Sheila was about one and a half years old. I was clearing up the caravan after lunch and granda suggested he took Douglas and Sheila (in her small pram) to the harbour and sit at the swimming pool till I arrived. He was noticeably upset when I saw him and it seemed the brake on Sheila's pram could not have been on properly and the pram with Sheila drifted off the harbour on to a moored boat, maybe about 20 feet below and turned upside down. Granda managed to get her still in the pram safely up on the harbour again which could not have been an easy task but sheer willpower must have helped him. Sheila was unaware of her narrow escape being young but granda was very distressed. I was horrified and did not sleep properly for ages. That was the end of granda walking the pram. The spooky bit came about when I got a letter from mum a few days later saying she had a horrible dream involving Sheila in deep water and to take care. I had to sit down when I was reading the letter as it was so uncanny . It still puzzles me as mum was not the imaginative kind of person and would not have written such a letter without a lot of thought. She was truly amazed herself when I told her what had happened. It changed the way I perceived things for a while but George being the down to earth sort of person he was then said it was pure coincindence but MY mind is always open!!

After we spent our two weeks in North Berwick we made our way up north to Arisaig for a further two weeks. We had a larger car and caravan by this time so life was more comfortable although pulling a larger caravan on the narrow roads of the Highlands was not always simple but George was a good driver so we managed without accidents. Drunk locals were fairly common in those parts so we had to be careful. How they managed to drive their vehicles always amazed me although their vehicles landed in the ditch fairly often but it never phased them and they just sat till someone rescued them. It was a way of life.

Arisaig and the surrounding areas was a great place to spend a holiday when young kids were around but I could never live permanently in the Highlands. The scenery is magnificent when the weather is good. It confounds me when I think back on how I managed to keep Sheila going in nappies (she was nine months old). I do not even remember this part of our holiday so it has not left an impression on me. Just put it down to being young and fit. We did most of our shopping in Mallaig which was about two miles away. Just a few shops and fish fresh off the pier which did not even smell fishy being so fresh. Hitchhikers were common on this road but we did not usually stop for them as the car was fairly full. We did stop once on leaving Mallaig for two girls who looked rather forlorn and did not realise that they had lots of luggage hidden out of sight so we had to help them load up and crush them in to the car. I well remember how disappointed they were when we dumped them off in Arisaig, They had hoped to get to Fort William. No more hitchhikers after that.

We spent future holidays in North Berwick and one I well rermember when Douglas was eight years and Sheila Four years. Within a few days of starting our holiday Douglas developed Chicken Pox and the Health Department insisted we moved to a far corner of the field even though Douglas had about six spots in all – a very mild case and he was not feeling ill. We got fed up being segregated and decided to make for

Arisaig which was isolated enough. Unfortunately Sheila was

infected and her case was entirely different as she was covered in spots and quite ill. After sleepless nights and Sheila feeling progressively worse we decide to return home and abandon the holiday for that year which proved the right decision as she took much longer to recover.

We bought our first house at number 16 Windyedge Crescent in Jordanhill in 1959 which was an end terrace of four houses with a large garden and fairly recently built. The previous tenants were immigrating to Australia. We sold the car and caravan to help us get the deposit and ease our way to property ownership.

I missed them both but having our own house after ten years was magic with all the extra space and just nice to have our own space. We did not lash out on lots of new furniture but we had our own living room furniture from Foxbar Drive. However we decided on a new G plan bedroom suite for our room as I think George felt he owed me that after sleeping in a put down bed in the living room at Foxbar. After a few years we managed a new suite for the living room so we were on our way.

Douglas continued At Bankhead School in Knightswood as he was settled with friends there and was happy. It was about a mile walk but he called in for Ian who was two years older than him at Foxbar Drive on his way to school. His Aunt Jessie was highly amused on morning when Douglas burst in saying 'Lamumba's' dead. She asked him who Lamumba was but Douglas had no idea and had only heard it on the radio before he left our house and liked the name. From what I remember he was some kind of African chieftain.

Sheila's school days began at Jordanhill School which was fairly near us with no main roads to cross. It was fee paying at the time but the fees stopped a year or two after Sheila started. The main aim in Windyedge Crescent was to gain a place in Jordanhill School so Sheila fulfilled this thus pleasing the residents no end so she had the usual parade in school uniform before leaving for her first day at school. This was one of the customs of Windyedge I did not like. A very close community where everyone knew all about you, very friendly but claustrophobic. We settled in quite well nevertheless and George built a garage adjoining the house and also a porch at the front door so we made our mark on it. I was friendly with Margaret Pringle, mother of a chum of Sheila's and we attended a Country Dance class in Knightswood Community Centre once a week which I enjoyed.

Lesley was born on 23rd September 1963 at home with the GP in attendance. She was born at 8.40am on our 14th Wedding Anniversary. As you would guess most of the neighbours knew before I did that a baby was born or about to be as they knew the doctor's car so it gave them a bit of excitement that day. As births go it progressed as it should during the night. The midwife came at midnight and kept me 'entertained' with her various deliveries, some easy and some difficult and with deformities which was just what I wished to hear. We were in the thalidomide era and deformities were beginning to show. I thank my lucky stars both for Lesley and ourselves that I was not a pill taker although I had morning sickness and those pills were being handed out freely but my GP had doubts about them so the decision was made for me. I was certainly glad to see a normal child at the end of it all. I enjoyed the home birth as I had both a midwife and a doctor at the birth but I think the midwife should polish up on her conversation pieces.

By the time Lesley was six months old we were thinking of moving house to something a bit larger' George was not entirely happy with the structure of the one we were in having thin walls and basic appearance although he had improved it greatly by adding a porch to the front door so despite the fact that there was room to build on we decided to move.

We finally moved to the house we are still in which had been bombed during the war and had to be rebuilt to pre war regulations which meant it was brick built with solid walls between all the rooms, bathroom and a cloakroom which we knew would be useful. It had been rebuilt in 1949 and two elderly ladies owned it so there was no damage to fittings but everything was brown and cream paint but that could be remedied gradually as funds were available. It had a lovely coke fired Rayburn cooker in the kitchen/dinette which heated a large part of the house. We kept it for a number of years till we got fed up clearing the clinkers out and went over to central heating which took me a bit of getting used to as we always had a lovely coal fire in the living room but central heating won the day in the end. Our dog did miss the Rayburn as he always lay in front of it so was totally confused at first till he found another warm spot.

I failed to mention that our new house was at 40 Eastcote Avenue so it was only about a mile away from the one in Windyedge Crescent and was still convenient for Sheila who was at Jordanhill School but Douglas moved to Hyndland School which did not plese him much. We were now living in a house which had a walled garden and I felt hemmed in for a time as the other house was a bit too exposed but soon appreciated the privacy of using my back door without being in full view of the neighbourhood. George was happy with the move the house being solidly built and all the rooms having brick walls. Our house was one of six houses rebuilt because of land mine damage during the war so it had to be built to the specification of the war damage commission. George continued with his studies and built a wee office in the large loft which

 he escaped to periodically. Escaping from his wife and three children could have been very nice at times which I reminded him of occasionally. He did work hard and passed all exams which helped provide us with a healthy pension in later life so will say no more.

One of my hobbies was Country Dancing so I made off twice a week in the evenings and also some afternoons to help keep me in trim. Sometimes wonder now if all the pounding on wooden floors was responsible for the disabilities I have in my eighties. I did Yoga for a number of years and Keep Fit classes and thank God I did for I certainly could not do any of it now!!!

George and I still liked the cinema and thanks to my dad for his child minding we managed to fit that in. In the 1960's we sailed a dinghy at Rhu on most Sundays which kept Douglas fairly happy which was a bonus as he was not easy to entertain.

This is the end of part one as there are many individual stories on my computer relating to aspects of my life for anyone compelled to read them.

Part 4. Sarah and I   1949 – 1959

This is an account of myself and my mother-in-law but in as nice a way as possible as she is not here to respond. To those close to her she was Granny Barr but her name was Sarah so that is how I will refer to her.

Being a newly married very young girl and living with mother-in-law under the same roof may seem like a recipe for disaster to-day but emerging from the dark 1940's with acute lack of housing gave us little option.

I would have found this story difficult to write when George was alive but sadly as he is no longer with us I cannot cause offence to him as he was fond of his mother as siblings should be. However I know for sure that I was top in the 'pecking' order and with his support we survived our ten years with Sarah and she still seemed sane when we left. It is without question not an ideal way to start married life but that is how it was after a world war.

Sarah lived alone in a three bedroom semi-detached house in Knightswood after Jessie and Rennie, her daughter and son-in-law moved into their own home and George had come out of the forces and paying all the bills of the council house so it seemed logical for us to move in. I do not remember any great discussions about this arrangement or how Sarah and I would rub along. If my memory served me right we took it for granted. I was a sort of quiet and agreeable young girl in those days and had never come across a mother-in-law before. My own mother had a few doubts but who listens to their own parents at that age.

My close friend Winnie was married to Don and rented a room in Scotstoun from an acquaintance of Winnie's mother so we visited them regularly. I saw it as an ideal situation and pictured George and I in a similar set up.

Foxbar Drive seemed fated for me however and George and I occupied the downstairs area of the house which consisted of two rooms and a kitchenette and Sarah lived upstairs in two rooms with the bathroom which of course was shared by us. One of the two large cupboards on the upstairs landing was converted into a wee kitchen with a two burner electric stove which would scare the living daylights out of Health and Safety officers to-day especially with Sarah who was well known for leaving cookers full on and disappearing to do something else. Her mind worked on many things at the same time. I am baffled now how this was allowed to be even thought about. Maybe all the traumas of the war we had come through melted our brains. We all seemed pleased with the division of the house and it never burned down but Sarah invaded our part frequently which is another story and a source of annoyance to me on many occasions.

There was a large garden which Sarah treasured and she worked in it all summer leaving wee bundles of weeds here and there for others to shift. She was not a tidy worker. In later years Douglas partially demolished her garden by beheading her dozens of beautiful tulips which were her pride and joy and he kindly handed her the beheaded tulips. It was one of the few times I have seen Sarah speechless and I had the grace to feel sorry for her but as Douglas was only three years old and not fully aware of what he had done there was nothing to say. When she recovered Sarah said plenty and cast it up to Douglas for years but in a nice way as she got on well with children but she had some peculiar ways of talking to them. In later years when Douglas could speak they had some amazing conversations as Douglas had an answer for most things as did Sarah.

To get back to my story – Before we married the house was re-decorated and new curtains, furnishings and all that. Sarah of course wanted new curtains to match ours which I suppose was ok Without my knowledge she went ahead and chose the material which I did not like and had them made to save me the bother by her way of it because I was working all day. MISTAKE NO 1..........I have a feeling that George was in cahoots with her here as I know he paid for them so this got my blood flowing a bit faster and I probably went in a huff for the want of anything better to do. I was not living there at the time as we were a few months off getting married but reality was beginning to set in. However our marriage plans still stood after some discussion.

George and I did go together to buy on hire purchase two large chairs, a table and four dining chairs which more or less filled the room. Sarah would have liked to have been involved but I put my foot down there so one up Nancy. Not for long though because George had decided to get loose covers made for the two large chairs (remember I was not on 'site') Of course I came to the conclusion that I was being shut out as I did not want covers for the chairs and I was sure that Sarah had also been involved in this decision which raises the blood pressure a wee bit MISTAKE NO 2...........
This all seems rather trivial now that I am putting it down in writing but I was young and going into my first house with a

new husband and this soon to be mother-in-law very much on the scene which was becoming problematic by the minute. We got past all those niggles and after all I was busy arranging a wedding and seeing life through rose tinted spectacles so maybe more forgiving but also showing another side of the 'quiet wee girl' by showing that I had a voice and realising it would have to be strong to compete with Sarah. In 1949 Women's Lib was probably thought of as a Liberty Bodice which had been recently worn by women and men were on a bit of a pedestal (their time was coming) At this time Nurses and Teachers had to leave their employment when they married and find another job who employed married women. This was about to change in the not too distant future fortunately when women realised they were as good as if not better than some men and about time too. I continued working after we married in a top class flooring firm in Clydebank who fitted out all the large liners on the River Clyde and I loved my job as a Wages Clerkess plus a lot of other things as you do in a small office. I f I had stayed at home looking after my husband my suffragette Granny would have risen from her grave. Also the mental picture of staying at home with mother-in-law around was not appealing.

Unfortunately as I had half expected Sarah made mistake number 3 by having a meal ready for us when we came home from work at 5.30pm I had been planning a nice solitary meal with George and showing off my cooking skills and she had intruded in my space shattering my dreams. Maybe she had the best of intentions but not in my eyes at that time of my life. A cook later on in my life would have been very welcome but that never happened. It took a long time to dissuade Sarah from intruding in our domain and looking back it never really happened as she was often decidedly visible.

I must explain here about Sarah's life with her sister Mary in their childhood. Being abandoned by their parents for reasons unknown they were fostered out at an early age by the Social department to a farm near Beauly in the north of Scotland where they were treated appallingly having to work on farm with no shoes or sometimes underwear except when it was known that Social Workers were visiting and they would then be given proper clothing and all would seem well. Atrocious treatment on two young children and I am sure it had a lasting effect for a lifetime. Sarah occasionally opened up and talked about her time in Beauly but she did not dwell on it. She was a strong character as I think she had to be as her sister Mary was a quieter type and Sarah probably looked after her. They were at the mercy of farm workers such as ploughmen so someone had to be strong. However Mary fell foul of one of them and became pregnant, Archie being the result of this encounter. He grew into a lovely man and looked after his mum in later life. Their working life was in service in large houses where Sarah was a cook. When I say Social Workers I doubt very much that they were called that in those days. It was probably a Department of some kind in the days they called a spade a spade. So much for progress! Those experiences in childhood made Sarah defensive and wary which I found hard to deal with in my youth. I suppose I made mistakes but this is part of the maturing process. Sarah did not have many friends and relied on family which was poles apart from my own mum who had a wide variety of interests outside the home so this was foreign to me and a big hurdle to overcome if I ever did.

For a year or so after our marriage we had an Alsatian dog called Flash which George bought as a twelve year old with paper delivery money. George and Flash were very attached. He was an elderly dog who took up residence in our small hall along with an umbrella stand and the outside door always open as no one would argue with Flash. Getting past him was difficult especially with a load of washing but he just opened one eye and let you get on with it. In winter he occupied the rug in front of the open fire and no one argued with him. He was put to sleep when he could no longer walk the vet coming to the house and George and Archie staying with him Sarah and I went upstairs to her quarters to console each other till the deed was done, Sarah was also very fond of Flash but was her usual stoic self and said that it had to be. We all missed him but I did not miss the sheep's hearts that Sarah cooked for him as the smell was awful.

George and I took our tandem to France in 1950 and had a great holiday touring around in good weather and flat roads which were important to me on a bicycle. George took more than his fair share of the pedalling on the tandem as he reminded me more than once but admiring the views was also important. We had no problems getting Bed and Breakfast and it was not too expensive as France was sort of recovering from the war. We found the food amazing not forgetting the wine. The highlight of our trip was a visit to Follies Bergere in Paris for George. By to-day's standards pretty tame though. For the records we took the train from

Glasgow to London and then London to Newhaven to Dieppe so our cycling started in France as there was no way I was cycling the length and breadth of Britain. Paris was my aim where I did some shopping needless to say. The only downside about France were the unfenced fields and bulls wandering around giving us the eye. George declared that my cycling vastly improved when a bull was in sight.

Not long after we returned from France I suffered my first panic attack which took me completely by surprise. It just seemed I was at my work normally and enjoying life when this horrible thing struck me and I was so confused and thought I would die. It entirely changed me from what I had been into someone who could not go out the front door and if we did try to go to the cinema I got to the door and refused to go in. We had a few attempts but the same thing happened and I am sure George was as confused as I was and I know it must have been hard for him as we do not have the benefit of experience at this time in our life. Sarah's attitude was as I expected and told me to pull myself together or George would look elsewhere so that helped a lot I don't think. In her mind she probably was trying to shock me into recovery. Funnily enough her words had no effect on me and I was feeling so low that if George had strayed I would have been unconcerned but I Totally knew that this would not happen and he always tried to understand.

I finally got medical help and also the constant and practical help of my mum who was central in my recovery by being with me most of the time till my confidence came back which took more than a year. I cannot thank my mum enough for the disruption I must have made in her busy life she never complained but she must have been more than pleased when I could stand on my own feet again.

Douglas was born towards the end of this episode in my life but he was a year old before I was able to cope on my own but it still was difficult. My salvation turned out to be Country Dancing which was held in the afternoon in the Community Centre across the road from the house so no travelling. I took many deep breaths and turned up at the class with Douglas in tow He was very well behaved and enjoyed the music and the attention from other dancers My first class was not easy but I got through it and as time passed got easier and I began to enjoy it. I met Nancy McKinnon there and we became friends. She also lived with her mother-in-law nearby so we had something in common.

A few years later I took up more classes in the evenings and also Keep Fit and Douglas informed the neighbours that his mummy went out dancing every night. A bit of an exaggeration but I wonder what the neighbours thought.

Jesssie and Rennie moved from Dumbarton Road to Corby when Ian was about five years of age. It was a New Town in England with nice houses and plenty of work for Rennie. This must have been a sad time for Sarah as she had looked after Ian from birth and suddenly they were no longer there but she never openly complained as this was not her style. One bonus for me was that she visited them fairly regularly for a month at a time so I was the Queen Bee for a while. The other side of the coin was that when they visited us at Foxbar the house was rather crowded but I also enjoyed their visits. Sheila was born in 1955, a fairly easy birth in Homeland Nursing Home with my own GP in attendance. I was now more able to face my panic attacks head on and learn to live with them but believe me it is far from easy. I now had two children to think of but still had problems travelling on transport. I convinced myself that the car which sat in the garden most days could be the saving of me and no more buses. I got my L plates and George was told he was to be my instructor. I do not know what his thoughts were but he agreed to give it a try. We got on quite well with the odd row when the gears clashed and he worried about what had once been his car and now I was preparing to take over. Before we got the length of a divorce a world oil crisis appeared in the Middle East resulting in a shortage of petrol. A decision was taken to stop all driving tests and that learner drivers would be allowed to drive on their own with special L plates. A great decision because it was much easier to drive without someone pointing out your failings and I had done all the basics of driving so as long as I found a quiet road the world was my oyster. Added to that it was noticeable that the other drivers on the road gave way to us learners and who can blame them. I know that this is a story about Sarah and I but learning to drive was a turning point in my life and Sheila was a wee two year old sitting in the back seat playing while her mother did reverse turns by the dozen. She did not seem traumatised by the whole thing but who really knows what damage was done.

We had now purchased a small caravan and spent weekends at Rosneath which allowed us to have time on our own. George had left his beloved Albion Motors and was working at Lennox College as a Lecturer in Production Engineering. At his suggestion he encouraged me to pick Douglas up at school on a Friday and with Sheila drive to Dumbarton to pick him up. I wondered if he had a death wish but he seemed confident enough in my capabilities to arrive safely at Dumbarton. Little did he know the state of my nerves on that first drive to the far reaches of Dumbarton. Twenty miles per hour was probably top speed and two very quiet kids in the back seat – scared to death likely. The sight of George coming out those college doors was euphoric and one of the highlights of my life. He was always so calm and matter of fact and not showing a great deal of interest in my mind blowing journey with his two kids. Little did I know that I would be driving all the way to Rosneath on those narrow roads in the coming weeks. His confidence in me must have been without limits.

Now to get back to Sarah and I ....

Jessie and Rennie had decided to move back to Scotland with their brood of three and got an exchange house in Johnstone. Rennie could not be separated from Partick Thistle any longer.

Sarah must have been very pleased about this arrangement as she could now see more of her grandchildren. I never truly knew Rennie's feelings about moving back apart from the football because him and Sarah did not always see eye to eye which I can appreciate as she was heavy going at times.. Rennie was the easiest person to get on with but Sarah always seemed to need an adversary.

George and I felt the need for more accommodation and asked Sarah how she felt about applying to the Council for a larger house. We were paying all the expenses of the house but it was in Sarah's name. George felt that the house if we got a larger one should be in his name but Sarah was not for that which did not surprise us. It left us no option but for us to buy a house which we did in Windyedge Crescent and leave Sarah in Foxbar Drive which she agreed to half heartedly.

The outcome was that Jessie and Rennie did not like Johnstone and agreed to come back to Foxbar Drive which suited everyone but Rennie possibly, but being the guy he was he did it for his family.

They spent fourteen years with Sarah and she died peacefully in her sleep in 1972 just as she would have wished.

In summing up my feelings are that Sarah sought the family and love she was denied in childhood but as a newly married I wanted to do things my way so there were obvious clashes. She once told me how to properly iron a shirt and ALWAYS iron the tail of the shirt. How I wish she was here to do my ironing at this stage of my life – there would be no arguments. As I have already said my own mum and Sarah were entirely different people so it was not easy coping with this new life but Sarah and I remained on speaking terms which is quite remarkable.

Part 5. Thomas Chambers 1893 – 1976

Sheila likes to keep me busy and she said she would like to know more about Granda Chambers so I will do my best…

Thomas was born in Lochwinnoch a wee village about ten miles from Glasgow to another Thomas Chambers and his wife Elizabeth. Those names are very common in our family so it can be rather confusing so you'll have to work it out. I was a small child when Granny Elizabeth died so do not remember her really. My memories of her are this lady lying in bed as I believe she had a stroke which left her bedridden. She may also have had a drink problem blamed on difficulties during the change of life but do not know much about that. She was known as 'poke' granny as she always had a bag of sweets for me when we visited. The other granny Hunter was known as water granny as she lived by the sea at Sandbank near Dunoon before moving to Torrance – very simple really!. She was also known for her lovely Scotch Broth which she cooked on an old fashioned range. Thomas had a younger sister Mary who was not very robust and lived in Canning Place, Townhead, Glasgow. She had various complaints but did not look after herself properly. Thomas seemed to deal with her finances etc. as she was not a capable person. She always had chocolate digestive biscuits in the house so that was good. Mary never married so there were no kids (as far as I know)

Thomas and Mary's upbringing was strict and very religious – church twice a day on Sunday, Sunday School and Boys Brigade etc. The Lord's day had to be revered. His father, according to Alastair's notes was Station Master at St. Enoch Station in Glasgow which seems a good enough job. He walked two miles each morning to Lochwinnoch station in all weathers to catch the train to Glasgow. I think it was a 7am start and finishing work around five or six in the evening so it was a long day finishing with the train journey and another two mile walk at the other end. The story goes that he suffered lots of sore throats so grew a beard to keep his throat warm and this seemed to work so maybe we should try that instead of antibiotics.

Apart from skating on Loch Winnoch in the winter I do not know how Thomas spent his young life apart from getting up to mischief like most boys do. He never spoke about his childhood days much, not like my mum who wrote it all down in a book. I believe they may have come to Glasgow at some time as the name Ronald Street rings a bell with me. Thinking it was the proper thing to do Thomas volunteered for the Forces in 1914 at the youthful age of eighteen. The government of the day strongly encouraged all fit young men to serve their country but he said that it was the biggest mistake of his life and led to four years of hell. He rose to the rank of Sergeant in a front line detachment so must have had a bit of responsibility and saw some horrible sights lots of his friends dying beside him and also knee deep in mud for months on end . He never spoke about his experiences often but he did mention of the truce that was called between them and the Germans on Christmas day and they played a game of football with the 'enemy'. Next day they were back to shooting each other again which made him wonder what war was all about and how senseless it was.

The trenches were lined with Corned Beef tins to strengthen them and this was also their main meals for the duration of the war. He had a lifetime loathing of Corned Beef and even during the second world war when it was prevalent again he never touched it.

The one thing that did haunt him was when he came face to face with the enemy and looked into their eyes and he knew that if he did not shoot them that he himself would be dead, so there was no choice.

In the end he was one of the 'lucky' ones and managed to come home after four years more or less unscathed, physically at least. Having been brought up a Christian he no longer believed in a God after his experiences. His dad tried to reason with him but Tom was a complete agnostic for the rest of his life.

He met Bessie soon after the war and she felt the same about religion being brought up from birth an agnostic. Her mother, being a widow with three children had her feet firmly planted on the ground and in her words did not believe in such nonsense. At least that was a good start from them and something to agree on.

When it came to their wedding Tom firmly refused to have a church service which distressed his father very much believing that they would not be truly married which in those days was shocking, however Bessie managed to make him realise that it was not fair to upset his father to such an extent and they finally agreed to be married in the vestry by the minister. Tom as was in his nature had the last word by telling the minister to make the ceremony as brief as possible as it was not his idea.

Tom had a stubborn streak in him and his temper fired up occasionally but he never showed it with me – I only remember him with affection. He punched a guy at his work for some reason or other and managed to get his 'books' from the firm I do not know the full story so cannot comment. There was an inflexible streak in him which showed at times. If things were not going well for me I was more inclined to get help from my mum as dad usually told you just to get on with it. His experiences during the war when he was such a young man must have had an effect on him but he probably thought it was 'soft' to talk about them men had to be men in his day.

Tom was rarely ill and I hardly remember him having a cold or 'flu, he was never off his work. I think he must have had a good immune system. In the late thirties he had a hernia operation and was in hospital for two weeks with a further two weeks in a Convalescent Home in Filey,Yorkshire at his Union's expense. Looked after their members in those days Seems incredible now.

Tom used a pedal cycle to his work in Hillington from Danes Drive rain or shine or even fog which was prevalent then. He was very fit!

Bowling was a hobby he enjoyed and most nights he could be seen at the Council Bowling greens just yards from our house. Then a wee pint at Blawarthill when he had the cash. He was regarded as a good player and won a few trophies It was a large part of his life for many years and only the bombing in the second world war interrupted it for a time. His eyesight unfortunately deteriorated which made things difficult for him and when he could no longer see the 'Jack' he knew it was time to give up which was sad. But he accepted the disappointment and as he said 'Life goes on and we have to make the best of what life throws at you'. He spectated for a while and still managed to go to the pub with his pals. It's not certain why he lost his sight but blamed it on sand running into his eyes in the desert. But who knows. Gardening gave him a lot of enjoyment and in his latter years he continued with this even though he had little sight. He once said to me that the day he could not look after the garden they could carry him away in a box and that was how it happened.

As kids Alastair and I were not allowed on the front lawn as my mum said 'in case you break the grass' He was very proud of it and fed it on a regular basis but he still had brown marks on it. The neighbour through the wall, Bob Hay, seemed to have a competition with Tom as to who had the better lawn – all a bit childish.

Hitler really gave them something to think about in 1941 when he blew their gardens to smithereens with a bomb. Tom's garden hut with contents, cold frame which he made and very precious plants and of course the precious lawns were no more and it was a case of starting again when we returned to our house. Just thankful no lives lost and garden was returned to its former perfection with lots of hard work. He grew vegetables instead of so many flowers till the end of the war which must have benefitted us.

Mum's brother, Alex who was unmarried lived with my Aunt Mary (mum's sister). He worked for Babcock & Wilcox in Renfrew who thought very highly of him. He was a clever guy even a bit of a genius, not in this world at times it seemed and entirely engrossed in his Electrical Engineering subjects. As a small child he could not come down to my level so I was a bit in awe of him, all our conversations ended in him explaining one thing or another that I never understood.

Tom enjoyed his company though and there was many a discussion in our house about politics or more usually wirelesses (radios now). The arguments became quite heated but they enjoyed them and were firm friends. Alex built his own wirelesses which seemed to me just a lot of wires and Tom would help him. I remember talk of the Cat's Whisker, whatever that was and the horrible oscellating noise that came from this bundle of wires, but this was a good result as it meant that they 'had a connection'. I did wonder why it was called a 'wireless' though as it was anything but. I remember a cupboard in Aunt Mary's house which when opened spilled out yards and yards of wires. He drove her to distraction at times but she was a very quiet, even tempered person which was just as well.

Tom could turn his hand to most household jobs, probably from necessity as money was not available to employ anyone. He got plenty of practice when we returned to our house as all the rooms had to be decorated from scratch. George learned his decorating skills from Tom and was always grateful for his help.

The authorities wanted to demolish our house but Tom insisted it be repaired as we would get back home sooner. We could have had a nice new house but not until after the war was over. It was like living in a builder's yard when we came home but we had to put up and shut up.

Tom retired when he was sixty five years still a very fit man , he had his garden and the bowls to go to but it took a bit of adjusting for mum as she had the run of the house all those years but that happens in every marriage. My parents however did not get on with each other at this stage in their lives so this must have made things harder. He also walked our dog Juno the beagle every morning on the dot of 11am as I was in part time work so this was a help and it gave him an aim in life. He also walked Bramble the poodle before Juno's time but he was put to sleep for biting when he was eight. I did notice that Juno was putting on weight and could not understand it and after dad died she regained her figure again. He always thought I did not feed her enough as she was constantly hungry but that is just how beagles are and I can only think that he brought food for her. Juno loved him!

My mum adapted by going out to her various committees and social events and more or less had her own life but was always home for mealtimes. She had lots of good friends which was a bonus and one of her great joys was the Citizens Theatre which she attended very often with a friend Mrs Gaffney.

Mum died in 1973 and we thought Tom would be unable to cope as his eyesight was almost gone and he was quite hopeless with housekeeping. He discovered Pot Noodles which he raved about and seemed to have them most days and he actually thought that he was cooking. He soon got tired of them and went on to tinned soup which was a novelty to him as mum always made soup. He came to us a few times a week for dinner and also to Alastair in Milngavie. Eventually, after a lot of persuasion he had a home help who tidied up and made his lunch and he got to like her which was a relief.

Jack Reid his long time neighbour was very good to him and called in each day with a coffee and he also had our phone number so all that helped Tom to stay at home.

He gradually found the walk to our house each morning a bit of a strain and the hill at Mitre Road which I never noticed (I do now). He still came in the morning for Juno but just let her out in the garden and he had a wee seat before going home.

Tom also did quite a bit of child minding for us when he was fit which we appreciated. Mum also helped but was often tied up with her pursuits whereas Tom always was available.

When George, Lesley and myself were in Blackpool for the September holiday week-end in 1976 we returned to find that Tom was very ill and confused. Our family doctor admitted him to the Western Infirmary but I am not quite sure why he deteriorated so fast but a circulatory problem was mentioned and he died in Gartnavel General Hospital ten days later.

He was buried at Cadder Cemetery beside mum, his dad and I think his mum and of course wee baby Tom.

Apart from the time he spent fighting in the 1914-18 war, which he deeply regretted, he had a good life mainly but he

reckoned he lost four young years of his life and for what? At least he survived to tell the tale when so man
y others did not.

When the 1939 war broke out I never fully realised how he must have felt with only twenty years between them. His only remark was that it would be an entirely different war which it was.

He was a good dad and although we were not too flush of money there was always enough and he worked hard but mum did the rearing of Alastair and myself he was the man of the house as men were in his generation………….

Mum probably got the last word when he told her that he would like six children and she told him to look for another wife as she was no breeding machine!!

Good place to end here……..

Part 6. Our Retirement

Some look forward to it some dread it and some accept it as part of life but retirement comes to us all eventually.

This allowed him to wind down gradually and being fit kept him part of the working population for a little longer doing the job he loved. It also brought extra income which is welcome.

In between the working spells we would take long walks with the dog and visited various parks around Glasgow. When the weather was suitable we took a car run to the coast and enjoyed the sea breezes. Life was good and I settled in to having a husband at home full time although at first he was inclined to suggest alterations in the way things were done in the kitchen but I completely ignored that and he soon gave up. For all his many years of engineering he never managed to fathom out the washing machine but perhaps a hidden agenda here.

Reaching retirement age and being quite fit is an achievement in itself so we looked forward to many years of activity. I had my own pursuits such as Country Dancing, Badminton (amateur), and swimming. George was happy walking the dog and he became well known in the area. He was good at DIY and would not trust a tradesman in the house which caused problems when he became less able. His garage was a workshop with loads of tools and often a bit of a mess but he knew where everything was and he spent many happy hours pottering. He served an apprenticeship in tool design in the Albion Motors and always had a love of tools. It never fails to surprise me why some young people feel they have to go to University when they leave school even though they may not have the intelligence. George studied till he was in his fifties and further improving his qualifications and always learning but not always through University..

Talking of George and his studies takes me back to 1974 when I had recently lost my mum and to help fill the gap I decided to brush up on my secretarial skills by taking a Course at Clydebank College and the prospect of working outside the house again. George was always keen on education so backed me by helping at home and with Lesley who was eleven years old. Sounds great but turned out to be one of life's experiences. One of our lecturers was a head case and had no idea how to teach. She came from another college I believe who gave her a good reference to get rid of her. She taught typing which I was fairly knowledgeable about but for beginners it was a disaster. To cut to the chase after various complaints to those above to no avail one bright spark in our class suggested we walk out every time Mrs Hope (unfortunate name) came in. We all retired to the cloakroom and this got the attention of the powers that be who told us we could not do that but we did. One time we got the head lecturer who was amazing but they told us she was not always available as timetables were arranged.

George was not impressed by our actions at Clydebank College and advised me to watch my step as he had a number of colleagues there and walking out was not appropriate but we thought it was.

However I got a bit fed up spending so much time in the cloakroom and also George was at a critical time in his career so for the good of all I left Clydebank College and all the problems and took a secretarial course at nearby Anniesland College which proved more successful. George never said much but I know he was pleased I was no longer causing him worry.

The hours were more suitable at Anniesland College so George got off the hook walking dog and looking after Lesley et cetera so he must have been pleased to get back to his own routine if he was being honest. Also I was no longer helping to cause a stir at Clydebank College. There was nothing else said about furthering my education after this episode.

Part 7. Lesley 2016

January 2016

I never thought for one minute that I would be writing this story but I do know that at my great age nothing should surprise me so here goes…………..

Lesley and Iain's marriage is hitting the rocks although it seems that it has been many years since it was a true marriage. It came to a head when having a family meal recently with Lucy and Kirsty on the eve of Lucy going back to London to continue her studies. It was about Lesley being asked by Iain to get him another drink and for some reason he started shouting and swearing at her to the embarrassment of all. Probably he had over much to drink but still no excuse to behave in this way.

After this episode Lesley decided enough was enough and told Iain she was leaving the marriage. I was not at all surprised as her vibrant personality had changed and she had to get it back. Iain does not see why they have to split and puts the blame at Lesley's feet which is far from the truth as he has many issues he will not admit to and Lesley has had to put up with. Difficulties lie ahead but she has the support of Sheila which she will need and of course myself even financially or otherwise.

Living in his own small world Iain blames Lesley for the split and does not see he is at fault in a large way for their problems. .We will live with this as no amount of talking will convince Iain otherwise. I have to be careful what I say here as Iain is dad to Lucy and Kirsty and they will have their own thoughts which I respect. They are in the midst of the split-up which is a very disturbing time for them as Kirsty is sitting her Higher Prelims which is difficult enough without the extra strain of their parent's marriage breaking down but those events never come at the right time and we have just to get on with it which Kirsty is doing admirably.

Lucy will be in London for the next six months completing her Pharmacy course so she is not seeing things first hand but is in regular touch by telephone and all the other gadgets available to-day but it must be hard for her. She has her own life now and must get on with it as I am sure she is doing in her usual exemplary manner.

Lesley feels that Iain is not playing fair at the moment and is secreting money away probably from gambling so let us hope this is untrue as Lesley has paid most if not all the mortgage and other bills from her wage since they bought the house and never got into debt. Her clothes have also been thrown out of the wardrobe so she has brought them to Eastcote Avenue and said nothing to him. She will now bring other items to my house as he seems to like playing mind games.

For some reason Iain would like the marriage to continue but he is certainly not going about it in the right way by his actions. I see Iain as a manipulative person with many issues and as far as Lesley is concerned the sooner she leaves the better.

Going through a marriage separation is no easy matter as George and I found out when Douglas split with Tricia. Iain's moods change from day to day if not from hour to hour. He likes to be in control and at the present moment he is not so Lesley gets the flack which is nasty at times. She decided at the beginning not to join him in verbal abuse so has tried to ignore insults tossed at her and concentrates on the time she will get her own flat but I see the effect it is having on her and would like her out as soon as possible for the sake of her own health. She has gone from a happy person to one with all the cares of the world and I hate to see this. Sheila assures me she will do it at her own time but it is hard to live with so no choice. I feel that I have never really known Iain as he was always distant so I thought we were just not on the same wave length. I know now that it was part of the problems he has but will not admit to.. His aim from my point of view is that he is set on hurting Lesley as much as he can and she does not deserve this.as she has put up with unpalatable situations in her marriage. The first came only a year after their marriage when Iain's shops went into bankruptcy. They lost their house and lived with Iain's parents for some time which was a poor start to a marriage especially when Lesley never saw it coming. From that day on Lesley was the financial figure in the marriage and had to learn fast.

12th February 2016

Lucy has had a few days in Glasgow from her placement in London which is her first visit since learning of her parent's marriage problems which must be a difficult situation for her but she is an adult now and I feel sure she will deal with them and also be some comfort to Kirsty who has been on the front line and seems to be surviving. She had Lunch with her dad which would have pleased him but I think he expected more. However she decided to stay at Hector's house which was a wise decision. I had a visit also which was much appreciated as her time in Glasgow was so short and she had a lot to deal with. Her time in London is hard work but she seems to be enjoying the experience of it all.

22nd February 2016
Iain's antics have at last to my great relief forced Lesley and Kirsty to leave Broomhill Drive. They will stay with me till a rented house becomes available. He sunk to a real low by cutting off power to the house resulting in no heating (in winter) no shower in other words no facilities. She 'phoned Sheila to say she had had enough and would she help her to leave. We were expecting this so no surprise and I was so relieved. She had to see her doctor as she had left prescription tablets in the house. One look from the doctor and she was signed off work indefinitely which was the only decision she could make. None of us realise how difficult it has been for Lesley dealing with Iain as she finds it too hard to talk about it but she has now made the break which is a beginning only. I feel that Iain has not accepted the fact that their marriage was not working or he was putting his head in the sand and hoping it would work out in the end but this will not happen as Lesley has finally made the break when she could stand no more of Iain's silly and often scary behaviour. Lesley and Kirsty will stay with me until a suitable rented flat is available which should be quite soon. My thoughts are especially with Kirsty who had to leave the only home she has known at seven in the morning taking whatever possessions she could for the moment. She is studying hard

for Higher Prelims and I sincerely hope this will not put too much pressure on her.

24th February 2016

After two weeks living at Eastcote Avenue when I got lovely meals made for me Lesley and Kirsty are moving to a rented flat for a year at Randolph Gate financed initially by Mum (and Dad's) bank. When her money comes through she will manage on her own but meanwhile she has her own space with Kirsty and hopefully get back to her former self in time. This is a massive state of affairs for all of them but as time passes it will be for the best.

Lesley and Kirsty love the two bedroom flat which also has a very large lounge area and kitchen.

Sheila helped them move in with added assistance from Andrew, Kirsty and a few others including Hector, Lucy's boyfriend who is a lovely guy. I only met him for a short time but was impressed. Lesley kept away from Broomhill Drive which we thought was a wise decision

In the meantime the lawyers are working to get a settlement which will no doubt take some time.

Iain still plays his mind games even with Lucy and Kirsty. He seems to have no thought for the fact that they are studying for difficult exams and is all consumed with his own problems which will drive his children away if he is not careful. Meanwhile   Lesley is back at work and very happy in her own house with Kirsty. Lucy would like to rent a flat like it with a friend when she finishes her stint in London so she was obviously impressed. Kirsty has said to Lesley that she has forgotten all about her home in

Broomhill drive and feels she has always been at Randolph Gate so I am so pleased that she has settled in happily. She has not a strong relationship with her dad but this seems in my eyes to be down to her dad as he has been too wrapped up in himself instead of having a bond with Kirsty. She is such a clever interesting person that this seems sad but it is her dad's loss in the end. Lucy on the other hand spends her time in London at the moment so has a different perspective about the separation of her mum and dad. This must make things difficult for her at times but I hope she gets on with her studies without too much worry as she will look back on this year in her life as time well spent with all the new friends she will meet and the sights and sounds of London.

I have always tried to be open minded about Iain but I can no longer take him seriously and will not forgive him for the way he treated Lesley playing mind games and forcing her from the house she had put so much into over twenty five years mostly in a loveless marriage. Leaving in the early hours of the morning was a huge decision but had to be taken. Time has proved it was the correct and only option. I feel sorry for Lucy and Kirsty but I am sure they will eventually understand.

May 2016

I am winding up my stories as my eyesight is not good and it is becoming more difficult to use the computer.

There is nothing more to be said about Lesley and Iain as they are now officially separated and things are settling down' She is staying another year in the flat at Randolph Gate as she is happy there. Lucy is moving to her first flat soon and is very excited about it. Both the girls see their dad regularly so that is as it should be.

As for Lesley I am pleased to say that I have never seen her so happy so another marriage hits the rocks but no regrets

Part 8. 80's

MANS REAL POSSESSION IS HIS MEMORY

IN NOTHING ELSE IS HE RICH

IN NOTHING ELSE IS HE POOR

Making Lunch is still within his capabilities, which suits me very well and he can also do dinner as long as the instructions are on the packet. My legs give in later in the day so I appreciate my dinner being served up.

A few months have passed and making meals are becoming more of a problem such as finding where utensils are kept and reading instructions on packets. His co-ordination is not good and I no longer leave him alone in the kitchen since he put a plastic jug with peas in the oven instead of the microwave. He did not realise that it was wrong which was more worrying.

Judy still has her twice daily walk but George has fallen or tripped a few times and no wonder, as the pavements are such a mess. He has to get out as this is his only pastime apart from crosswords and Sudoku which he is a bit less interested in now but finishes Sudoku most times. !

Turning on television is becoming quite a problem for George now and he gets frustrated not being able to follow instructions Seems to have lost co-ordination a bit. It never fails to surprise me that he always remembers when The Weakest Link is due on. Maybe he fancies Ann Robinson!

He now uses a walking stick which surprised me as he was so against them a short time ago. The fact that he has fallen a few times made him realise that a stick would support him and he admits to being unsteady on his feet and benefits from it. One thing in his favour about George is that he wears so many layers of clothes and is well padded when he falls.

Now January 2012 and in the intervening time I have acquired a Lap Top which has rather filled my days. I never thought that I would be sitting here putting stories on a computer at my age. It's all thanks to Sheila and Lesley for their patience that I have managed in some way to master this machine and it does help to divert me from day to day situations. George is utterly amazed that I have managed to cope but I know that he would have enjoyed the computer age if things had gone differently for him.

Judy has developed arthritis like myself but still enjoys going out and still gets her twice a day walks but we do not feel guilty about the lack of long runs for her as she could not cope. George and his memory are not good, pretty awful at times, so walking Judy is his only aim in life apart from sleeping more often. He always finds his way home which is good. If he went out of his routine walks I think he would have problems but he still manages to collect an order at Bradfords the baker and also prescriptions at the chemist. The shops know him as 'George'. I have found that he manages alright if he goes for one thing at a time and on his own as I no longer encourage him to take Judy with him which would be too much of a distraction.

Looking after his own medical care is way beyond him so I put his weekly medication in a day to day box but every morning he checks what day it is. If he is on antibiotics it's a bit of a nightmare as I have to hand them out one at a time and hide the remainder in case he takes more. He has no idea when he took the last one. One plus is that he manages to shave, shower and dress himself as I doubt if I could help him much.

George no longer cooks but still washes the dishes although not very well and quite often have to be done again. I miss this part of his help and he now needs supervision constantly and would never cope on his own. He is completely wrapped up in his own world and it can be very distressing trying to get through to him about the simplest things This can drive me crackers at times and the difficulty of living with someone with no light in their eyes or responses is demanding but I know that if the position had been reversed George would have done his best for me so no more to be said.

Having a few problems getting up and down stairs I turned my thoughts to a stair lift which the more I thought of it the more appealing it was so I had a number of quotes all in the region of £3000. After much deliberation involving the family as well I decided to have a word with Andrew, our Jack of all Trades man. His thoughts were that maybe the exercise was quite good for me and suggested extra handrails which have worked very well and George also appreciates them It also looks less cluttered than a stair lift would have been. Happy all round! Andrew also enlarged the step at the back door and fitted a handrail as I felt insecure going out the door with washing etc. Lo and behold however on Boxing Day George managed to fall IN the back door and badly injured his shin. Must admit I tripped in Sheila's door last summer an d bruised my knees which did not help my walking at all.

Being on holiday Lesley came to our assistance and brought proper dressings round immediately and dressed his wound which was quite extensive. Her view was that best to keep away from all the bugs picked up in hospitals plus all the hanging around waiting for the staff clearing the drunks. So handy having a nurse in the family.

She continued to professionally dress his wound every other day for at least four weeks which was the time it took to heal. He called her his 'Angel' so that was her nickname for a while. After that healed he developed an abscess in his mouth resulting in a tooth extraction which of course had to be done by the dentist as Lesley's talents did not cover that. All quiet at the moment apart from his usual problems.

At this moment in time, February 2012, George spends his day walking Judy, morning and afternoon for about half an hour each time. The remainder of the day he spends sleeping and eating which is an important part of his life (he enjoys his grub) Sometimes he does not feel like taking Judy out but when I suggest other arrangements he says he is ok. When he is out he seems to enjoy it and it keeps him from sleeping in the chair and being selfish gives me time to gather my thoughts

Lack of communication on his part is very evident now and if I do not speak, neither does he so the day passes silently with him in his own wee world. Watching this deterioration is having a depressing effect on me at the present time but I try to counteract it by reading, crosswords, and also the computer which I am so glad I purchased. I have even been known to clear out a cupboard on my really bad days. How's that for an existence? Going for a long walk once helped me in stressful situations but that is no longer feasible as I would not get far. Judy is some compensation as she follows me everywhere.

This is not a 'poor me' attitude but a fact of how our lives have changed and if I were 100% fit would cope a lot better. Some days are more difficult than others and hard to keep going when I don't want to. Some appreciation from George would go a long way to help but that is now beyond him although he very occasionally says how grateful he is but that does not happen often.

For me, writing is therapeutic and helps me to accept the situation as it is (sometimes) , We are an elderly couple and have to expect problems but this does not always help nor does the fact that others have worse difficulties. I have to find my own solutions to our situation as everyone is different. Being ignored by someone you have known from a very young age is the toughest part. I have adapted a bit as I know this is something that cannot be changed and no fault of his.

I cannot imagine how it must feel for George being hard of hearing and also not knowing what happened ten minutes ago. He does not seem too stressed about it but he never was one to talk freely about his emotions so who can really say. He does get upset when he forgets where items are kept which happens regularly.

A feeling of doom comes over me when George decides to open a conversation as it usually means that something has happened such as falling, medicine running out, light bulb blown, television not working or some other such thing. This happens quite often when I have settled down to have a rest so my patience is stretched. To have a nice conversation about something in our past that had pleasant memories would be good but I do not see this ever happening again. It was a total surprise one evening when he came in from the kitchen where he had been watching television (or sleeping) and said that he must tell me about the great film he had been looking at about Lancaster bombers from World War 2. He rarely watches films as he finds them hard to follow but this one seemed to stir up some memories and I was sorry I had not recorded it. It has been erased from his memory by now.

On 6th January 2012 our first great grandchild, Layla, was born to Ben and Linda who live in London and naturally she is a perfect wee girl. We get loads of pictures through Face Book so this is one advantage of having a Laptop. I try to keep George informed about what is going on in our lives but it is hard as I have to explain every time who Ben and Linda are so it depends on my mood of the day how well informed I try to keep him.

Dr Woods of the Glenkirk Centre at Drumchapel Hospital arrange for George to be taken out every second Wednesday in order to give me a break which it does but would be nice if it was weekly. George visits various places like Shipyards, Museums, Hampden Park and also the Lomond Shores which he enjoys as the two ladies who accompany them are extremely nice. If they do not go out they stay at the Glenkirk Centre and play Board games or watch films of days gone by. They also have quizzes which must be interesting. They have afternoon tea wherever they are and George is amazed that his cup of tea costs £1.45. Has no idea of the cost of living now. Times are difficult at the present time but my thoughts are that GP Surgeries should take more responsibility for their elderly patients who have difficulties at home instead of referrals to Social Work Departments and Carers. My experience so far has not been beneficial as I have been invited to a five mile walk in the country or coffee at Anniesland Offices which is all very nice maybe for younger people but when we reach our eighties bits of the body start to mal function and I personally would find it not worth the effort to go to Anniesland far less a five mile walk (if only). I have what the doctor feels is Spinal Stenosis which is not as serious as it seems so I'm told but does make walking difficult.

Regular contact by GP Surgeries, say once a month, even by telephone to find out how we are both coping would be helpful by knowing that there is some sort of support when we require it. Afraid it is not going to happen as it is not an ideal world and not much money around with people like us living longer. It did happen in the past believe me. Contact occasionally could help the carer feel more visible.

I have been with the same GP Surgery since I was nine years old and seen lots of changes . My family, granny, mother and father and all our children have had excellent attention from the Surgery so have no complaints about that. At one time we attended the Doctor in his large house at Balshagray Avenue where his 'surgery' was a room set aside in his house. There was a personal touch which can be lacking now when you visited him in his own house with a room set aside for his surgery. He was acquainted with all your family and probably knew all their business also. On the credit side we have a nice surgery now more like a small hospital with high tech machines helping us to live a longer and better life. Have got a bit distracted here but that's my 'rant' over.

Getting back to George now and our uncertain future............

March 2012 and the days are getting longer, summer my favourite time will soon be here. We started planning for our long caravan holiday about this time of year but regrettably George has no memory of those times which we did enjoy touring around with our then dog Freckles our first Springer Spaniel who was a great traveller fortunately. Our destination was Worthing on the South Downs where we usually spent three weeks, that being the permitted time to stay on Caravan Club Sites. We knew the couple who ran the site very well and it saddens me that this dreadful illness has denied George all those lovely memories and also from my angle I have no one to share those memories which is very painful..

Another incredible event is that George has entirely forgotten the sudden death of Freckles from a road accident outside Victoria Park which he witnessed and was distraught as we both were. It happened in 2000 when she was eight years old and as you can imagine he felt a lot of guilt and sadness at the time. It took him a long time before he could pass the area where the accident happened but the memory now is completely wiped out which in some ways is a good thing.

The loo brush appeared beside the dishes on the draining board of the sink recently and as he washes the dishes I wondered what on earth it was being used for – considered washing the dishes again till I realised he had been cleaning the walls of our pantry which get a bit mouldy at times. Must admit that he and the loo brush made a good job of the walls but left job unfinished.

Each day brings differing problems which I try to solve in a reasonable way which is easier said than done some days depending on my mood and own troubles. Laborious trying to get him to understand situations with the hearing problem and memory problems combined. Sometimes silent screaming helps!.

George takes a run on the No. 44 bus into Sauchiehall Street fairly often as he gets some enjoyment from this and always seems to manage to get home ok. I doubt very much if he would manage on any other bus service as familiarity is important to him so it would lead to confusion. I suggested he stay on the bus to the terminus for an extra run but he was not impressed. He sometimes takes a look round Marks & Spencer before coming home but this could be because when he was well a number of years ago he and I went in to town on a Friday and he dropped me off then parked the car. We met up after an hour or so in Marks & Spencer when I had completed the shopping. We did this for many years so it obviously jogs his memory. I get time on my own for a few hours which is nice and helps me gather my thoughts. Would not like it all the time but for a few hours – great!

Our Great Granddaughter, Layla came to introduce herself with Ben and Linda recently. They called in on Linda's mother in the Newcastle area and also managed an overnight stay at Lesley and Iain's. It was a quick tour of the relations and we had a lovely meal at Lesley and Iain's house. Very nice seeing Layla in the flesh so to speak as she is a happy baby and gave us a few smiles so we had lots of photos taken. Although Facebook is not my favourite pastime we do see photographs of Layla.

Judy has had an operation for a large lump on her chest which I'm pleased to say was benign but is confined to the house and garden for a period of time. George has had his routine of two walks perday interrupted and he has to be persuaded to go out at all. It is important that he keeps mobile but is stopped by many people asking where his dog is so he was well known in the area. He is not deeply motivated to do anything apart from sleeping although still shaves and showers himself adequately. Seems to like his own wee world.

It is now May 2012 and since Judy's operation in March she has developed a lame back paw which still keeps her confined to the house and garden as her walking is not very good, doing a bit of 'bunny hopping' when she walks which the vet is worried about. He feels that the weakness is coming from her back rather than her paw which is not good news.

At this moment of time George has pills for cellulitis as well as the other usual ones and as he is not able to sort them out himself I have to do it as well as various pills for Judy. George gets antibiotics four times per day and Judy gets antibiotics three times per day as well as a few others and she fights taking them so times are difficult. Added to this are my own pills for blood pressure but have coped so far without mixing them up.

Unfortunately Judy is losing ground as she has now been diagnosed with kidney problems along with extremely high blood pressure. Attending the vet two or three times a week and feeling the extra pressure but Sheila and Lesley help when they can. Judy lost the use of her rear legs at the vet when on a visit so the time had come to make a decision as it is sad seeing such an active dog the way she is. She was put to sleep on 23rd April and the vet felt sure she had a spinal tumour so it was the correct decision. Goodbye to dog No. 9 in our marriage and also the last as age is against us. Mr Snadden, the vet said that Judy was very special to him which was nice. She was financially special to him also.

George coping better than I thought he would as a matter of fact better than all the rest of us but he has still to be encouraged to keep taking walks.

Episodes of cellulitis continue annoying George and his legs have been quite angry looking so Dr. Marshall called in to see him and his opinion was that it is eczema which he has over his body and has to apply creams regularly which is very time consuming. On speaking to George the doctor seemed to realise the pressure I was under with one thing and another and my own mobility problems so arranged for nurse to call to help with the cream situation. This sounded quite good getting help but the nurse called in at 8.30am completely confusing George because it put him out of his routine. She called back once more then thought we could cope on our own and to be honest I do not do early mornings so agreed it may be best to manage on our own so Nancy in charge again! The doctor did suggest however that he would try and get him more time at a day centre to give me a break so Christine Thorburn a Social Worker whom I had already met and did not get very far with her would phone me to discuss things. Alas six weeks have elapsed and no phone call from Christine so no hope of any more time at a Day Centre in the immediate future. The doctor no doubt means well and tries to be helpful but little co-ordination between services as far as I can see. Lots of talk about help but nothing actually happens in the end. Probably

hope we'll die off before anything needs to be done!!!
Another afternoon to myself would have been nice but in the meantime I appreciate the services of the Glenkirk Centre who take George out for an afternoon once a fortnight which he looks forward to as well as myself and he looks brighter when he comes home by the fact that he was doing something and the two girls are extremely helpful.

Hope that I do not sound uncaring to George's predicament wanting more time to just be 'me' but that unfortunately is how things are. We have known each other since I was sixteen years which was very young. Seventy years is quite some time to be together apart from three years during the war when I was nineteen. They were traumatic times, many couples splitting up because of the uncertain times we were living in. My own parents had problems at this time losing their house in the bombing, rationing, two teenagers and blackout to contend with but I think the straw that broke the camel's back was granny living with us with dementia and not much help for mum – pure hell.

George and I never had any thoughts of splitting so we must have had something going for us. When we married we stayed with his mother for ten years because housing was in short supply. It took its toll on me latterly, we had a little 'blip' and I took the kids to stay with my parents for a few weeks as I was stressed out. It was resolved when we bought our first house and finally had our own space.

I would find it hard to cope on my own without George with all his problems after such a long life together but on bad days I do crave for time on my own (just a little). When we are young it is impossible to visualise the future and how situations can change so drastically.

June 2012

big changes about to happen and no social worker involved. George needs something more to think about and also he mentions the hill coming up from the park which he always took in his stride. We have now ordered a top of the range (of course) five wheel Motor Scooter which both of us should use as our mobility is not as it was. A test drive was arranged and the firm appeared with this handsome scooter. George was slightly wary and suggested that the scooter was for me which I agreed but suggested he had a run on it with the salesman. He was convinced that it would not be able to take the hill up from the Park so was taken to the hill and was amazed at how smoothly he reached the top. When he arrived back home he thought whole experience was fantastic so that was him won over. I enjoyed the test drive also but had already been on one at a Shopping Centre. It happened to be a lovely sunny day so that helped the experience. However we decided to order one and it arrives about the 19th June so looking forward to it and it will mean that George will get further afield and the fact that he has once more his hands on a mechanical device will please him. We paid £3891 for it £1000 pounds less than the starting price as usually happens when buying anything. However we will be the first one to own this particular make of Scooter in our area so the firm were keen to get our business so if they sell any more through us scooting around in it we will get a bonus of £50 – if you can believe that.

One of the most difficult things about caring for George is that every decision in our life has to be made alone. In the past decision making was a joint responsibility, his input being blunt and to the point so I had often to use my persuasion to talk him round which I sometimes did. Let's hope that my decision about the scooter is the right one I sometimes feel I live two separate lives, his and mine. By far my biggest concern is the lack of conversation in my life and some days pass without any at all or very little. If my legs would allow me to go out more this feeling of isolation would be less troublesome but concentrating on what I CAN do gets me through most days so this I keep uppermost in my mind. George cleared the garage of old wood he collected from skips in the area, sometimes managing to pick up some really nice pieces of wood like walnut and teak which he used to make bird houses and wheelbarrows for plants. When he walked Judy and Freckles he kept an eye open for skips and if there was anything of value he returned with the car to bring it home. Sometimes workmen emptying a house would tell him to help himself so he did quite well over the years. However most of the good wood was used up so this was rubbishy stuff that was left and the Council took it away for us. Nice clean garage now just waiting for the Scooter which is being delivered in a few days.

I cannot believe I am saying this but I still miss Judy following me around everywhere I go, she annoyed me like heck when she was here and now I'm moaning that I miss tripping over her.

Monday 18th June and Scooter coming to-morrow morning right on the date they quoted which is rare. Been reminiscing as one is liable to do at my great age and thinking we started off with single bicycles, then a tandem, from there a Ford 8 second hand car pulling a trailer dad built with camping gear, then various caravans, motor caravan (VW) then for fifteen years or so gave Hotels in Gorleston and Bognor Regis our business. When Lesley no longer thought us 'cool' back to a couple again and more caravans, just myself, George and Freckles and touring the Country at a leisurely pace.

Who would ever have thought we would reach the giddy heights of a Mobility Scooter – speed 4 – 8 MPH. Maybe we should buy another on e and recapture our holiday with the tandem in 1950 to Paris. Could be interesting but I doubt there is enough time left so we'll settle for Victoria Park.

Watch this space for to-morrow!!!!!!!!

Knock on door 9a.m. still in bed but Mobility Scooter at door and George trying his best to find out what was going on at the door at that time of the morning. Delivery man was spelling out to George who he was and having a hard time but I got downstairs pronto before he keeled over (delivery man not George). After the usual explanations of the workings of 'Scooter' and what all the buttons and levers were for he left us to get on with it ourselves which is sometimes better as we have a good instruction book with plenty pictures of all the parts. George drove all around the garden which is pretty well covered in paving stones so ideal for a try out but dodging the flower pots, which he did.

In no time at all he was out the gate and round the block thoroughly enjoying himself and agreeing how good it was. Sheila took him to the park and she was pleased with how he was coping and enjoying himself. In a matter of days he went to the park on his own which worried me a bit as there is a main road to cross but he said he waited till it was completely clear before crossing. He was used to doing this route with Judy so knows it very well.

The one fly in the ointment is that on the dashboard are a number of buttons which you press for horn, lights, signal for going left or right, hazard which to me are rather useless when he is on the pavement. He was accidently pressing them and did not know how to press them off again so was coming along the road home bleeping, bleeping. I taped them up and it helped a little so I decided to 'phone the makers to see if they could disconnect them as he only required 'forward' and 'reverse' but this was not possible as it was a health and safety issue (how I hate that term). I contacted Andrew, my favourite technician, electrician and ex engineer on Nuclear Subs as I felt sure he would come up with a solution as he usually does when problems arise (except George). He has agreed to come and look it over to see what can be done.

Andrew very kindly came to-day and disconnected the offending button so no more bleeps from that We also covered up the other one and George had a successful run to-day with no problems. Peace now reigns once more.

Worth a mention that this guy Andrew I talk about has been a bit fly as Sheila informed me that she and Andrew are now an 'item' and have been for heaven knows how many years, nine I think. I would never have thought that this would have gone on without me being suspicious so I am not as smart as I think I am. No more to be said as I have been told to keep quiet about it!!! I am very pleased for them nevertheless.

Now July and for some reason I am feeling rather low and depressed. George has his walks and also a run in the scooter if the weather is dry so all is satisfactory with him which is good. But I am finding it increasingly impossible to engage with his brain which is exasperating. He has to be given assistance from morning till night in most things that he does, finding key of garage, key of scooter, hat and gloves the list goes on. I am in a grudging mood at the moment which makes me feel guilty but I know I should not but overwhelmed some days and even had thoughts of moving to place of care where my needs would be considered which frightens me as this is not on my agenda.

When one reads of couples like ourselves who have problems with one of them having to be cared for by the other and they are devoted to doing so it makes me feel bad to feel the way I do but how hard is it caring for someone who does not respond to you at all? That is the upsetting part plus my own problems. I am not placing any of the blame on George as he would not have chosen to be as he is.

I have to be optimistic that this resentful episode will pass and serenity will return.

I think I may have spoken too soon as George has come downstairs saying that he has no cream for his dry skin and I know that there two tubs in his room. It is 11pm and had a few attempts to assure him that there is cream in his room, feeling tired myself so get off to bed and postpone 'serenity' till later. This early stage of dementia, memory loss or whatever you like to call it lasts for many years where we just jog along and do our best helping and prompting the one who has problems but it eats away at the other partner who is constantly on the watch and knowing that things can only get worse and taking each day as it comes . I do not like the word Dementia as to me it means demented which George is certainly not. I often think that a small area like a caravan would be ideal for George where all essentials for living are close at hand. He would find it easier to cope I know but from my point of view it could be hell on earth with no escape.

August now and got myself together a bit more, amazing how moods can change. George spends a lot of the day asleep and I often wonder how he sleeps at night. Decided after some thought to try and take George off his pills for depression. He was prescribed them years ago because he was a worrier and seemed to look on the dark side of things. With his memory as it is he no longer worries so I did not see the point of them and he agreed to try coming off them although ten minutes later he had forgotten our conversation. I doubt if he knows the meaning of the word 'worry'. We did it very gradually and also had a word with a friend of Sheila's who is a pharmacist and agreed with us as he takes other drugs for blood pressure etc. He has been off them for four weeks now with no apparent ill effects but I do feel that he sleeps less during the day and is slightly more aware of what is happening around him so any improvement however small has to be welcome. His day now consists of a walk of an hour, very slowly, for an hour (about a mile). He takes the mobility scooter for a run in the afternoon then another walk of an hour when he comes back. Not bad for an 89 year old. He has been known to add a run on the no. 44 bus into town as well on some days.

August 22nd and have been at doctor's surgery with George to have a wart removed – first visit to surgery in a long time. He was treated by Sister Stewart with Nitrous Oxide (?) and told to phone her if it had not gone in three weeks. She knows he is deaf so cannot use the phone plus his memory would never remember after three weeks. He never heard a word she said anyway but I don't think she noticed. We were ushered out in less than five minutes with 'bye George, 'bye Annie leaving George confused about when he was to come back again. The Surgery was deserted so I wonder what the hurry was. A wee card with written instructions was all that was needed and George would have pinned it up on his memory board. Wart Clinics being held monthly shows the demand and there must be many patients like George who attend. Not so long ago he would have been asked how things were health wise but no time or interest for some reason. The niceties of the past are gone so I am probably spoiled but feel that it does not take up much more time to say a few words. It would also have helped if Sister Stewart had sat opposite George when talking to him as the doctor does instead of giving him instructions while walking around putting equipment away.

Next morning he asked me if he had been to the wart clinic or had it been a dream. George gets confused quite often by dreams and reality. Lesley also gave us good advice and told us to put sticking plaster over the wart thus cutting air from it and this would speed up procedure. This method is used in Yorkhill Hospital where she works as a nurse so thank you Lesley and hope this will be end of story.

I have just been accused of drinking a bottle of wine each day by George who assures me he throws an empty bottle in the bin every day. Before the family start to get worried this is just not true, a glass I admit to with my dinner. Maybe he is seeing into the future if the pressure he sometimes causes increases (God forbid), He is probably getting confused by the bottle of lager he takes with his dinner, thinking it's a wine bottle. He thought I had bought a new ironing table to-day because it has a new cover. At least he is noticing what goes on around him! September 2nd and George is not having much luck, last Tuesday he took ill, more confusion than usual, fever and generally not well so doctor visited him and prescribed antibiotics for a suspected bladder infection. Left a bottle for urine sample which I delivered later on in the day. It smelled foul so no doubt what was wrong. As the day progressed George went downhill and became very confused and could not stand on his legs. Long and short of it was that Lesley was convinced that he should be in hospital so we went through the procedure of calling NHS out of hours doctor as it was eight o'clock at night. He came in about an hour and thought that he could be looked after at home but Lesley was very persistent that he should be admitted to hospital apart from the fact that I could not cope with someone not able to walk. After some talk between the doctor and Lesley he agreed to admit him to hospital but still felt he was not ill enough (don't know how ill you have to be). The ambulance came about midnight and Lesley's pressure to get him into hospital proved correct as he had a high grade infection and was put on a drip for dehydration and also for antibiotics. He was fairly ill for two days then he suddenly became the life and soul of the ward wanting home and also a Herald delivered to his bed each day. The staff on the ward were great and looked after him well. Unfortunately he was in a stroke ward as it was the only bed available When Lesley and I visited him on Saturday afternoon it was decided that he could go home as his bloods etc. were back to normal.

He said it was the happiest day of his life and Lesley swore that if he could have managed it he would have kissed the ground when he got outside. Said he was so bored as there was nothing to do all day. Has been quite well since he came home and been out for a walk, doctor 'phoned and said he would like to see him in two weeks to check his blood etc.

I had to stop George from collecting order from Bradford's the baker and also the chemist as he was putting life and limb and anyone else near him in danger by not crossing the busy motorway at the proper crossing and he did not seem to understand how dangerous it was. It is sad that he can no longer do this as he felt useful and the shopkeepers all knew him and helped. He still goes walks and I hope he takes care but would not be fair to keep him from doing this. As the weather gets cooler he is not using the motor scooter but this was to be expected. I have not ruled it out for myself so watch this space.

23rd September 2012
Our 63rd Wedding Anniversary but has very little meaning to George as he does not remember our Wedding. He has gone into town on his favourite No. 44 bus so that is his 'celebration'. Let's put it in verse:-
MISLAID MEMORIES
One more year for George and me
Now at 'sixty-three'
That special day I well recall
For George afraid it's not at all

May seem unfair and wee bit sad

But still our George and still our Dad

Old age is a bad habit and no-one as yet has written a book of rules about how harrowing it is so we make them up as we go along.

Let's not forget Lesley's 49th birthday to-day as she was born on our 14th Wedding Anniversary. She celebrates by doing a marathon Zumba and I think Lucy is with her so she can pick up the pieces!

As you can see I am celebrating by sitting at my Laptop which has been a great plus for me as it gives me some direction. Sheila opened her new kitchen last night by inviting us all round for a take away which was lovely and the grandchildren added to it by honouring us with their company.

Enjoyed my blether with Nan and Ishbel at Nero's café in Crow Road where we had Lunch in celebration of Nan's 80th birthday. Nan is the youngest of our group of five and unfortunately Anne McKirdy is now permanently in a Hospice so we do miss her. Nancy McKinnon disappeared to Largs many years ago and severed all connections from us for reasons only known to her. We three are left and meet on a fairly regular basis to keep in touch and have the usual laughs and moans. Nan and Ishbel are members of Broomhill Church which has an ageing membership so when we meet I always hear of someone dying or now in a Residential Home. We naturally hope that we will not go down the road of Residential Home but that will be for the future to decide and hopefully we will be able to stay in our own homes. This may sound a bit gloomy but it is a fact of life at our age and we do joke about it!

George was left with his own Lunch when we were at Nero's but I prepare it before I go as he has great difficulty organising himself now. He is always on edge till I come back home now which seems rather odd as he does not bother what I am doing at home unless preparing his meals. Sounds rather selfish, but it is the way things are and it is hard to take but no blame can be put on him as his mind no longer works adequately. His main contribution to the working of the house is bringing in the washing from outside and handing it to me at the back door – quite a help if the weather is cold. Some days the strain is worse than others and I feel quite vulnerable but in the end have to deal with the situation in the best way possible the worst part being the lack of normal conversation each day which is extremely isolating. I am trying to give an accurate account of our lives from day to day so hope it does not sound too carping as it is not meant to be.

I have been diagnosed with Spinal Stenosis which gives me a bit of bother as it has now affected my sciatic nerve which is very painful. The doctor referred me to a Physiotherapist in Southbrae Drive and Sheila accompanied me for my first visit on Wednesday (24th October). I feel that she could pick up on things that I may have missed. I am not expecting miracles but if it helps the sciatic pain I will be happy. I felt my visit was successful and she gave me exercises to do and I see her in another ten days. Her visits cost £45 but will be well worth it to get even a little improvement. I have no bones to pick with the NHS but it is almost impossible to get an appointment for physiotherapy the way the country is at present. I will continue with my 'core' exercises and hope for the best.

Almost November 2012 now and clock has been shifted so winter is now here. I think it is time to put the motor scooter to bed for the winter as George feels the cold so much I do not see him using it till the warmer weather, It takes him all his strength to go out at all some days but I know the feeling myself. Unfortunately I have to go out for shopping etc. but George is happy to sit in his chair and let life go on around him sometimes trying the Sudoku but mostly staring out the window and falling asleep. In the past I have tried to get him interested in reading and crosswords but when there is little memory left it does seem pointless when there is no memory to even remember the beginning of the last sentence he has read. The same applies to films on television as he cannot remember what he has just seen. Golf is the main sport he watches and I think it is because it is a slow game and so easier to follow. He also still watches football occasionally but I do not know how much he takes in as he quite often gives the wrong score at the finish of the game.

He was at Dobbie's Garden Centre with the girls from the Glenkirk Centre to-day but all he could talk about when he came home was how cold he was. I had a pleasant few hours to myself so that is the bonus.

Lots of birthdays fall this week starting with Sheila's on 2nd November then Lucy and mine on 6th November followed by Cameron on 9th November – quite amazing really.

November 4th, in middle of birthday season and was awakened by George telling me that he could not stop the bleeding. Morning is definitely not my best time so crept out of bed and looked in the bathroom, blood over the loo, on the floor and more or less everywhere but just smears so that looked hopeful.

Went cautiously into his bedroom and blood on floor and bedding but saw it was coming from his lower leg which he is inclined to scratch but denies all knowledge. Both his legs are very swollen and scarlet which have been for some time as he suffers from eczema which he puts loads of cream on. Being the morning I just stood and looked at the mess around me and cried which was really helpful but all I wanted was a cup of tea to wake me up. However I did hand him a towel to hold over his leg and got him sitting down thus stopping him walking around dripping blood everywhere. I honestly felt like going back to bed and pulling the covers over me but that would have been less than beneficial so I 'phoned Sheila instead – you know what they say about a problem shared! Sheila was along in less than an hour and by this time George and I had tea and toast so feeling slightly better but because of my own problems could not get down on my hands and knees to clean the mess which frustrates me a little. Sheila being Sheila took over the cleaning and changing the bedding in no time so outlook looking better. She then 'phoned Lesley which I had not done as she had a party for Lucy's birthday the night before and thought she may have been under the weather but Sheila thought she had long enough to get over it.

Being the professional that she is she said she would be round later with proper dressings for George as Sheila had already bandaged it to keep infection out. We are fortunate to have two supportive daughters nearby but I am not sure how they feel about that.

Lesley thought that dad's leg warranted a visit to the doctor which I arranged to-day and as luck would have it was at the same time as a physio appointment I had. Lesley agreed to take him to the doctor as she was on holiday from her work. He has special dressings which Lesley will put on when we get them from the chemist thus saving me a visit to the surgery. He goes back in a week for a check to see how his leg has progressed. George surprised me to-night by saying how helpful Sheila and Lesley were. I sometimes think he does not notice but obviously not true. Being 'me' I reminded him that I was with him twenty four seven but I doubt his brain managed to work out my quip.

This week has not been so great with George and Lesley has dressed his legs several times with special dressings which I will not even attempt to pronounce. He is also very listless and not keen to go out or do anything but sleep (and eat). On Saturday 10th November he had a shower before Lesley dressed his legs again and he came downstairs with blood dripping all over the place, obviously from scratching but as he insists he just rubs them with a towel. Lesley sorted out his legs and we decided to give him the antibiotics given to him in case it was necessary as his legs were very inflamed. Lesley then tackled the blood in the bathroom and all the rooms he had trailed through. His skin is thin and bleeds easily. All quiet again but we visit the Doctor's surgery to-morrow so Lesley has written a note explaining George's deterioration and asking for more help such as day centres as he only goes once a fortnight and he seems to benefit from it and I must say I enjoy the break.

It is coming to the end of November 2012 so all the birthdays are past. George's leg is improving with loads of cream being put on but the worry is when the covers on his leg are removed and he scratches again. He has an appointment with Sister

Stewart at the Surgery to to see how things are progressing and Lesley has written a note to let them know how much work is involved with looking after George at the moment and how worried she is about me having to take this on with my own problems. She has asked for more Day Care help and also considering help in washing him and putting cream on which involves his whole body but particularly his legs. The note from Lesley has had the desired effect and we have got things moving now.

I have always been wary getting help like this as I feel it takes away our independence but no option now as the memory problem is much worse and is very distressing so hopefully life will be a bit .easier. Soon Care Workers will be here and my hope is that I will be able to accept help and not feel it is an intrusion on our privacy only time will tell....

November 1st and George had a sorry attempt at making a filled roll for his lunch something he always managed to do even though he put HP sauce on all of them. He had no idea where to begin and had to back away eventually. There is nothing now left that George can do for himself except make a cup of tea. This puts extra pressure on me as all his daily tasks have to be monitored. Just wish I was more able physically to help him but that is not going to happen. So we hang on and do our best.

It is a very long time since I was sixteen and George was eighteen. We believed that the world revolved around us and seemed not to have a care in the world. It was a magical time and feels like another world now with no connection to the present time. Never for one moment did we imagine the year 2012 and striving to exist with one whose memory is consigned to oblivion and the other having to live with this grim fact. This illness is prevalent in society to-day and not only in elderly people so hopefully a cure will be found soon. Help is on the horizon now as from next Wednesday 5th November George will be receiving help in showering and applying his cream for three days a week in the meantime. Bluebell Care supply a service for what they call Personal Care and charge £14.50 per hour but hopefully we will be able to claim back £10 from someone who call themselves Direct Payment but this has all to be arranged. They will also take him to the hearing clinic at Gartnavel Hospital which he sometimes has to attend.

All this is alien to me as I like my independence but I know it will be helpful all round so it has to be and I will get used to it in time. Trying hard to remain positive.

There is also a vacancy for George in a Day Care Centre which is quite near but he will be picked up at 9.30am and dropped off at 3pm. This has still to be arranged but we should hear soon and George seems happy about it. He does not go out much in the cold weather so this will give him some stimulation instead of sleeping all day and will give me a break also. Although George finds it difficult to communicate I feel he realises I need time to myself and accepts those outings. . This is not associated with George and myself in our 80's but is closely concerned with us as it involves granddaughter Lucy and a break up with her and Jack her boyfriend of eighteen months.

She visited us to-day with Lesley and was heartbroken which was very sad to see. However no words can help her at the moment and no sticking plaster to mend it, we could only give her hugs which I hope helped a little. Just proves that at any time in our lives we can have stresses which we can only get through as best we can and maybe come out stronger in the end but I doubt Lucy believes that at the present time.

George has now met his carer, Joe, who will continue to see him three times per week to help him shower and put his cream on. He is allocated one hour and as it does not take an hour to shower he does some ironing for me also which suits me fine. George is very happy with Joe and seems to get on with him and vice versa so one problem solved at the moment. As for my own feelings in the change of routine I know it will take some time to get accustomed to 'carers' coming in to our house. For one thing I have to get up earlier and pretend to be bright and awake when I am anything but awake. However George does benefit so until he can get a place in a daytime centre I will have to carry on but from all I am told this should happen fairly soon then I will have my 'me' time. Once or twice a week would be adequate and also give him some other outlet.

George had Christmas Lunch with Lynn and Muriel from the Glenkirk Centre but was less than impressed when he came home. They were all talking at once and he could not hear much if anything so was not a successful outing for him as he was bored. They usually watch that he can hear what is going on by writing down things but being Christmas they were probably distracted. 'HAPPY CHRISTMAS'

We saw Dr Woods recently for an assessment and he agreed that George was in the early stages of dementia. This began in 2009 and proves what a slow moving horrible illness this is. I like Dr Woods as he is also on my side and assured me that he would hurry along a place in a Day Centre for him as he felt it was essential for both of us but will not count on a place soon as I was told that there was a place four to six weeks ago so nothing happens quickly.

Christmas been and gone now and back to normal whatever that is. I visited Sheila on Christmas Eve with Lesley and family and enjoyed the company. Ann Hilton was there with her family and never fails to give us a laugh. Lucy was there and is gradually accepting that her and Jack are no longer a couple but it is not easy especially at this time of year but she will get there like others do. Dad was a bit confused when I came home and had most of the lights on in the house probably looking for me I am all he has got so I suppose he has to make the best of it!!!   Will hesitate to leave him on his own again as he forgets where I am and even leaving a memo is useless as he would not read it. Gone are the days when he was pleased to see me going out….

Christmas day we spent at Lesley and Iain's and had a lovely meal prepared to their usual high standard. George coped well but Christmas means nothing to him and it is just like any other day. Maybe he has got it right and we are all mad during December.

George had a blood test recently (now 8th January) and our GP phoned to say that he wanted to discuss the results with us as blood count not perfect so we see him on Friday 11th January. He is not feeling great and sleeps most of the time so we will have to wait and see what transpires.

We have changed the hours of Bluebird Care to half an hour per day as carer thought that half an hour was sufficient time to shower and put cream on as George can still help himself a bit at the moment but this will probably change in the future but in the meantime we can save some money. Proclean Cleaners thoroughly clean the house once a fortnight so this is adequate and it is not necessary for Bluebird to do any cleaning. I have established a rapport with the carers now but naturally would rather they were not necessary but this will not happen. The trouble is at the moment lots of staff have gone down with 'flu so the carers change from day to day but this is inevitable.

I suppose it could be said that I was the official 'carer' of George although never in my wildest dreams would I have thought that possible. It is not a job I applied for but more thrust on me by circumstances. George or myself would not have chosen this to happen but you have to play the cards as they are dealt and hope for the best. Yesterday got me off to a bad start by a phone call from Drumchapel Hospital waking me from a sound sleep to give me a date for George to have an assessment regarding a body scan he is due to have because he seems to be losing blood from somewhere. I think people who work forget we "Oldies' do not rise early. It got me off to a bad start and in no time Joe arrived to help George get washed and dressed. I of course have to lay out all his clothing which is no mean task as George has a habit of 'hiding' his clothes and no one can find them. I could put them out the night before but George would probably put them on going to bed as he loves plenty clothes on. Having carers may sound great but I have to get involved to some extent when I would rather take things easy in the mornings. However at least George is clean! Without sounding inconsiderate I sometimes long for an unchallenging few hours when I can switch off.

The remainder of the morning was taken up by making soup and washing clothes as Joe thinks I run a hotel and wash towels every day as well as the pyjamas which have only been worn for one night. I now remove the towels and pyjamas from the washing machine when Joe disappears. This may sound trivial to those who are not 'carers' but believe me those small things pile up to make a mountain. Added to that are my own problems which make moving around very tiring and a husband who cannot begin to comprehend the obstacles to be overcome in looking after him because of his unfortunate condition. You will never believe it but we now have two walking frames and a zimmer in the house George has a frame with a seat for using outside and I have a frame with a tray to make carrying my dinner into the living room easier (I have bad habits). The other one is a slim line one for George using during the night when he has to get up as he was bumping into things and fell once so this helps. Our house beginning to have the appearance of a Nursing Home but at least we have the freedom to come and go as we want so what the heck! Talking of coming and going George never goes out now unless taken out by car but we will see what the better weather brings. My feelings are that he has become housebound and will remain that way as his walking is now very poor. The days of him taking a run on the number 44 bus to town are over as he would never cope with that now. How life can change in a few months.

I had a lovely afternoon with my friends Nan and Ishbel who live nearby. Nan phoned this morning to invite me to her house and I told her I had to do some shopping as my cupboards were bare. On reflection however I realised that it would be more sensible to get in to company for an hour or two and ignore the shopping. As luck would have it there was indoor bowls on the television all afternoon so George spent his time watching the wee white ball going from end to end. I left him a note saying that I would be back between 4.30 and 5pm. When I came home at 5.15 George mentioned that I was a bit late (the working of his mind never fails to amaze me) Is he taking the 'mickey' out of us? Lesley repeatedly tells me to put dates on my story so this is 25th January 2013

I recently received a text picture of Douglas, who divorced us many years ago, and I presume his wife whose wedding we were not invited to. Ben seemed to get the picture through face book I think ,the point is that the image was so like George it was unbelievable but I had a sad moment or two knowing it was too late for George as he has no appreciation of the relationship between him and Douglas any more. Makes me realise how sad it is that he has no contact with his sons or his lovely granddaughter Layla, also Sheila and Lesley and families I gave up a long time ago trying to work out how his brain works but I feel he will be the loser in the end. That was a hiatus in my story so back to George and I and life in our eighties.

Our visit to Drumchapel Hospital with George about his blood count and general health went quite well and the feeling is that he remains on iron pills and continues as usual but have his blood checked in a few weeks again. The family all agree that this was a satisfactory outcome as we did not want him to have to go through invasive tests.

The cataract I have had for some years is now at the stage when the optician advised me not to drive until I have an operation so Lesley is running the car till such time as I can grab it back from her. Hopefully this will not be too long as Lesley is doing a bit of pushing stressing that I am a carer and require the car to get around because of my own disabilities. I miss the car but have gone through worse so another stage in my life. I may even begin a friendship with the wee motor scooter laid up in the garage for the winter months. I doubt very much if George will use it again. I wonder if they make tandem versions of them!!

One of the supervisors from Bluebird Care came this morning to wash and dress George because they are short staffed. Elaine always pushes me to keep nudging Direct Care to help pay for George's care. At first I thought she was being very thoughtful but I have come to the conclusion that it could benefit them as well as I would be encouraged to take ten hours per week as against the half hour per day we have at the moment. No one knows what the future will bring but at the moment I am satisfied with the half hour per day and to tell the truth I am glad to see them go nice and all as they are. Still have my own thoughts about the Caring system. Money wise we are managing very well since my legs do not allow me to wander around shops. I have sussed out the internet so do some shopping there but still prefer personal shopping.

February 11th will hold a place in my memory as a very traumatic event happened when Lesley, Lucy, Kirsty and myself had Lunch in the local eatery McMillans. I I got a part of my toasty wedged in my throat and it would neither go up or down. In some distress Lesley tried the Heimlich technique but only partly worked. A gentleman who was dining in the restaurant came forward and grabbed me round the waist and literally lifted me off my feet applying the same method as Lesley. He obviously knew what he was doing and after three very hard pressures on my ribs and three hard thumps on my back the offending piece of toasty became dislodged to everyone's relief. By the time the paramedics arrived I was recovering but we can never thank that gentleman enough and I do not even know who he was as he disappeared when he saw that I was ok. If he had not been around the outcome could have been so different. This is a lesson to us all that we should learn the Heimlich technique and be able to help on such an occasion. Sore ribs were the only after effects but a small price to pay for what might have been.

No word about the Day Centre at Munro Place that George was promised a place in many weeks ago despite Dr Woods and the Social Worker assuring me they would try to hurry it along. The excuse was that they were installing a new kitchen but that was a few months ago so should be finished by now. I was promised a phone call in January but I have heard nothing and it is the same old story, strung along and nothing happens and we are left in limbo again. I really wonder what Social Workers actually do they certainly do not keep in touch with the people they are supposed to be helping. All the wonderful leaflets that are left with you telling you that you are not alone and the help there is 'out there' seems a load of nonsense as I have never seen it yet and I AM alone apart from the family but certainly not from Social Services. A neighbour two doors along whose husband had Parkinsons had the same experiences and I thought that she was overstating the situation but I know now she was not. They are all extremely well trained on the telephone when you do manage to get in touch with them and promise all the help but that is the end. All I really want is for George to have one day per week in a day centre which would be helpful to him and give me time to myself but he still only has two to three hours every two weeks and it looks like it will stay that way.

George and I were brought up in a world poles apart from 2013 and no mobile phones to call home or cars to run a taxi service for teenagers., we learned independence quickly so I am sure we will survive without the 'help' that fails to appear.

One good invention about this age is the laptop which gives me a chance to put down in writing all my moans and groans!!!!!

It is now the last week of February with longer daylight and bulbs appearing in the garden so something to be happy about. Maybe this year we will have long summer days and I can read my kindle on my swing in the garden I could have two good eyes by then. Our nice young man, Michael, keeps the garden tidy and will tackle most jobs that need doing. George is attempting small walks with his walking frame after the long winter inside so that is a good sign.

Halleluiah it is now the 5th March 2013 and George has a place in the Munro Place carer centre starting on Friday 15th March. At present it will be for one day per week but after a month he will have two days. Two sort of scruffy looking social workers interviewed us and one of them looked as if he could have done with a place in Residential himself but he told me he was 61 years old and had been with Munro Place for twenty years. He was slightly indecisive, dropping leaflets and waffling a bit but who cares George has got his place twice a week which is just what I wanted. I think George will accept the change alright and settle down quickly. Our social worker's mother is in Munro Place and loves it so that is recommendation enough. I had a strange reaction to George getting a place at Munro Court which surprised me. My first date with George when I was sixteen was at the Vogue Cinema close to the care centre and we walked along that road many times to our favourite cinema until it was finally demolished to make way for a B&Q store. Memories came flooding back of our very young days and such carefree days. It seems idiotic but the memory plays strange tricks on us. I got through a great pile of ironing that afternoon and life returned to normal whatever that is.

I have decided to ditch Bluebird Care in favour of Cordia which is Council run and free of charge. The service we get from Bluebird is nothing exceptional and George has about four carers in a week so no continuity as they promised. Also there was hope that we would get help with the payment to Bluebird from Glasgow Council but with money being so tight at the present time our chances of getting help are very low so we are in the process of changing over at the moment but not for financial reasons I just felt not getting value for money. Maybe 'out the frying pan an into the fire' but I hope not.

We have four large plastic bins that are parked in our garden, one for papers, one for garden rubbish, one for glass and one for household rubbish, all different colours. George was always the bin organiser, cleaning it regularly and putting them out on the designated day, all very efficient and orderly. Alas times have changed and they now drive me mental. EVERY day George asks which bins go out in the street for collection and I repeat EVERY day that they do not collect till Wednesday so they go out on a Tuesday night. I have tried to do the job myself and sometimes manage it but George is so programmed he rarely forgets. After all if he asks every day it is bound to happen. He does not even recognise the colours of them so that is a double whammy.

To-day was the green and brown bins so he put the brown bin out early on in the day and I told him to wait till night time till the last of the day's rubbish was put in it before putting the green one out but this afternoon I asked him if he would close the gate as it keeps foxes out but of course he passed the green bin and decided to take it with him and put it out. After our evening meal he asks me where the green bin is. My stress levels were rising rapidly and after all it is only a bin and worse things going on in the world. To-nights rubbish was eventually dumped in the bin (hopefully the green one). Later on in the evening I was managing to unwind decently but it never lasts long. George suddenly appeared from the kitchen and asks (yes you know) "WHAT DAY DO THE BINS GO OUT"? This is a sample of our daily life. There is only a football match with two foreign teams on the TV and no golf which he likes watching so I told him he would have to watch the football to-night. He has a comfortable chair in the kitchen and he likes the heat also. His parting shot was that if he did not like the football he would keep me company. No answer to that one!!! It has now become clear that George does not retain anything in his memory and it is a case of only telling him he is going out at the last minute. It is a demanding existence with no happy ending and trying to keep positive is the only way to approach the future. I know I have said it before but in this illness one person is incapable of adequately living their life and the other person has to do it for them as well as trying to have a life of their own. I know that women are renowned for multi-tasking but I never thought it would be in this way.

15th March2013
To-day George was picked up by a mini bus and taken to Munro Court Day Centre at Anniesland Road. The last hour has been spent explaining to George where he was going and when he would be coming home. I think we went over it about twenty times so I don't know how much of it was in his mind as he left. Watching him being accompanied to the bus and the passengers already picked up smiling at him some with vacant faces made me feel very sad that his life had been reduced to this.

Emotions can suddenly be knocked sideways at such times and leave you vulnerable and my thoughts turned to the many times he had enjoyed walking Judy along   Anniesland Road near Munro Court in more carefree times. It is not wise to dwell in the past but it does intrude from time to time.

George will benefit from his times at Munro Court and hopefully help to stimulate a part of his brain still active and we will both benefit from time to ourselves which we have not had in the last few years. Coffee now, feet up and a read of the paper and Sudoku.

Have said adios to Bluebird Care from yesterday 19th March and hello to Cordia Care and Karen the new carer who is in her early fifties, pleasant and efficient but the one drawback is that she comes at 9am. Mornings are not my best time as I have said before but there is no charge for this service as it is run by Glasgow Council so I will have to go along with it. On the plus side Karen is more mature than the twenty year olds at Bluebird which I feel is an advantage to patients like George. Nothing can change what has happened to George but we can do our best to get the most suitable care for him and this seems to be happening. Dare I say such a thing but stay positive Nancy………….

This is the Easter week-end, the clocks go forward which I like so summer is approaching and when the weather gets warmer I may even have a run on the scooter. Sheila took me to Braehead Shopping Centre to do a bit of shopping and I used a scooter which is supplied free and apart from bumping in to a few things in M&S (my eyesight of course) it was a successful day and I arrived home remarkably fresh and no sore legs. Coming to terms with using mobility aids takes a lot of getting used to but the alternative is rubbish also so 'bite the bullet' and accept how things are.

A letter has come in for a preliminary examination at Gartnavel Hospital for my cataract operation so it should not be too long now before my sight is being restored.

George is now at Munro Place care centre on a Tuesday as well as Friday so this is good and he seems to be quite happy there as he tells me how caring the people who look after him are so that is good news. His observations were that he liked it more than he disliked it so that is good enough for me having known him for so many years. To be forthright about it I'm sure he enjoys all the attention he gets there which is not always possible with me.

The previous paragraph is a bit of a non-event now as there haves been sudden changes to our set up at home. George took suddenly ill with sickness and the 'runs' on 25th April and was removed to hospital where it was also discovered he had a chest infection. The following night Sheila, Lucy and myself were struck down with a similar bug which for Sheila and I lasted for seven hours. Lucy seemed to be a bit less affected which was just as well as she had a visit to London planned to see a pop concert which she managed to go to. How different for Lucy's age group when we recover much quicker. During the long night of the runs and sickness I was sure I would die and I did not care. As you can see I recovered eventually in some ways thanks to the phone calls from Sheila during the night as she was suffering also. George was improving in hospital but was not allowed to leave hospital till I was well enough to look after him which meant he was in for five days and of course we could not visit him. Sheila and I were both very weak but Iain paid him a visit one afternoon. Lesley was in Blackpool for the week-end so she was out of the picture

We eventually got a confused George home although I was struggling to manage but with the help of Sheila and Lesley making meals we emerged from the nightmare.

We all agreed that George brought the infection probably from his care centre as times were just right. It was the only place he had been to and he was the first in the house to take ill. We are not laying any blame as bugs are everywhere and who really knows where we get them. Munro Court is a lovely place and have very caring staff but my feelings were that we had been lucky not to have had such a bug in all our long lives and it was too risky an option for a near ninety year old to let him continue there. The other motivation was that George was not all that happy there as he said he felt like a bit of a 'turnip' sometimes as he could not hear what was being said. When asked he said he would rather be at home if there was a choice. My administrations cannot be so inadequate it seems.

His social worker is arranging for a 'befriender' to visit him as she agreed that care homes were not for everyone and George responds well to a one to one situation as he can hear better so this could be the answer. I can also go out when they visit which is a possibility. I enjoyed the few hours he was in the care home which relieved the stress but not satisfactory if it is replaced by other worries so here's hoping we've got it right..

13th May 2013
Lesley came across this lovely but sad poem which seems so appropriate to my story................

DO NOT ASK ME TO REMEMBER
-----.

Do not ask me to remember
Don't try to make me understand
Let me rest and know you're with me
Kiss my cheek and hold my hand

I'm confused beyond concept
I am sad and sick and lost
All I know is that I need you
To be with me at all cost

Do not lose your patience with me
Do not scold or curse or cry
I can't help the way I'm acting
Can't be different though I try

Just remember that I need you
That the best of me is gone
Please don't fail to stand beside me
Love me till my life is done

Unknown author

I thought this nice poem painted a word picture of how I see George and his problems. He is very insecure at times and does not like to be left alone for too long. I can be away fifteen minutes and he thinks it is hours and he becomes confused and worried. The days are long gone when he was quite pleased to see me going out the door for a while I can only try my best to be supportive.

Memories come back to him however as not long ago he asked me what happened to him when he was demobbed from the army and where did he work. I explained that he returned to the Albion Motors where he had been serving an apprenticeship in Engineering when he was called up for the forces in 1944. He remembered being in Egypt for two years but had forgotten what happened when he came home and it seemed to prey on his mind. I told him he was in the Royal Corp of Signals for three years and when he came back we just fell into the way we were before his call up, a bit older and hopefully wiser. He was amazed that I could remember all that had happened and found it hard to grasp how I managed. It made me realise that he appreciated what a good memory was which I found upsetting. To think he could forget all those letters he wrote and received in his time there.

31st May 2013.
A wee moan or two from me now as the past few days have been something of a bad dream to me. It's hard to pinpoint the cause, small possibly insignificant events which all add up to a huge problem. I almost envied George his dementia and the twenty four hour care he gets which shows how low I've sunk. My own problems are many which is to be expected when we reach the age of 87. My coping mechanism had failed me for some reason and I feel trapped in a situation I never wanted or expected. A carer plods in at 10am to wash, cream and dress George, twenty minutes in all and she is a very nice person the remainder of the twenty four hours is down to me. I appreciate he was at a care home twice a week for some time but the last chapter explains why he left. A befriender was to be put in place but that has not happened yet. George sleeps a lot and is not a bother but situations change rapidly at times. Being alert to someone's needs constantly is getting to me.
I was hoping the cataract operation I have had recently would allow me to drive again but this may not be a possibility. A few more years of independence would have been nice but at my age I have done quite well so no room for complaint. My eye operation has not made a vast difference so bit disappointed.

Sheila and Lesley help with the shopping but I do feel a pest at times remembering my own parents when they had health problems. Also my gran who stayed with us for two years in a small two bedroomed house. How mum survived the war years, two teenagers and a mother with dementia in such cramped conditions I'll never know. She must have been a Saint!! Knowing those facts does not make it any easier for me unfortunately as we all have to find a way round our own obstacles.

Most of my problems that I had in the past were solved by a long walk in the fresh air, it never seemed to fail but lack of mobility rules that one out. At this time of year I loved planting out my tubs in the garden but Michael my gardening boffin prefers planting in the soil. One thing to be thankful for is that we can afford to pay Michael to look after the garden and he does it well but I will still try to have my tub of begonias in front of the kitchen window with the help of Sheila maybe. As you may have noticed I am feeling more positive perhaps because to-morrow is the 1st of June and the start of another month, still with the same problems but hopefully a more composed frame of mind.

It is now only the 10th June and no great improvement, whoever said that old age is not for the 'spineless' knew what they were talking about and I get daily reminders of this fact. George is not aware of the reality of this most times but I am all too aware of the changes in our lives by the slow deterioration in George. I have had gout on my big toe for the last week and expect it to last for another week before it finally goes so this is making life that bit harder at present Gout pain must be one of the worst..

I have increased the Proclean cleaners who clean the house to once a week now as the dinette where George has his meals gets messy with spilled juice and sticky fingers. This maybe seems trivial to able bodied people but a major trauma to me so hopefully I've sorted that problem out. We both were fortunate to get the top rate of Attendance Allowance which helps to pay for such things also the Teacher's pension that George receives through his work in teaching during his life which he studied hard for into his fifties but it has paid off now when we need it.

This next paragraph is 'comic cuts stuff' – it is now 17th June 2013 and I have a follow up at the hospital after cataract operation on 21st June at 9'15am and Sheila is taking time off work to accompany me. I phoned Cordia to ask for help looking after George for two hours as he gets confused when left alone. Cordia referred me to his Social worker Helen Jackson who according to the literature are there to help us at all times stay in our own house (good idea). Helen said to phone Cordia but I told her I had just done that and they referred me to her (Helen). I reminded her that someone sat with George for five hours when I had my cataract operation four weeks ago which she found hard to believe but it DID happen.

Back to Cordia and they assured me that George was booked in for only half an hour every day which I do know but this seemed an exceptional case. I did say that George only takes up twenty minutes each day so there is a ten minute discrepancy and they must owe us lots of ten minutes which could be added up. Slight pause here but no response from that.

Poor Helen getting another phone call from me and by this time I was about giving up on them all before my blood pressure went off the scale. Helen talked me round and assured me she would phone around and see what could be done to find a solution.

.

Lesley and I went to Marks and Spencer for the first time in three weeks as she has been celebrating her 50th birthday for the best part of a month recently so she is now completely knackered but getting back to normal living. She was chuffed that George said that he had missed her as we are inclined to think that he does not notice time passing.

Sheila ran Lesley and I to Dawn's at Airdrie on Saturday (12th October) as it was Jordan's 18th birthday. I thoroughly enjoyed catching up with all the relatives that I mainly see on Face Book and not so often in the flesh. George was left at home on his own for the afternoon as he could not cope with so many people around him who would all seem like strangers to him. Although I leave various notes about the house telling him where we are he does not seem to read them so it defeats the purpose. On one of his recent walks with his rollator two different people asked him if he had far to go so he must have looked a bit done in but he still enjoys the short walk and it is nice to think that some people still care.

I climbed my own 'everest' to-day when I took the scooter round the block not once but twice so how is that for progress? It has intimidated me for so long but maybe I am finally conquering it. Unfortunately the colder weather is coming in so it may not seem so attractive. I tell myself to get plenty clothes on and get out there so we will see what happens. I miss the car but no use dwelling on the past so on to the next set of wheels which undeniably are poles apart but will still get me to the wee shop at the garage nearby and make me less dependent. It will also widen my horizons by the fact that I can go out of the house for a short time when I feel like cracking up.

A few days ago life started as normal on rising but soon went downhill with small irritations from George which he was completely unaware of. I was working in the kitchen doing the usual boring jobs and getting more and more aggrieved and tired at his lack of understanding. This is part of life now but for some reason I felt resentful of him happily doing his jig saws without a care in the world. I had a melt down feeling sorry for myself, my coping mechanism failing me so I spent an hour in tears before phoning Sheila in her Lunch break and laying it all off to her no doubt making her sad as well. It all seems so trivial now that I have stopped feeling sorry for life as it is. The chat to Sheila on the phone helped and I am just sorry for those who may have no one they can call on. This lack of feeling and comprehension from people with dementia is the hardest part to accept but it comes with the illness. The chances are that George thought I was just having a bad day and not realise that he was the reason for it which is exasperating to say the least. .

22nd November 2013

Now back to as normal a life as I can expect and what is left of my brain was ticking over thinking of some hobby a person with dementia could tackle in the coming winter months when he will not get his wee walk that he enjoys. His early training as a draughtsman meant he was good at drawing and in Egypt in his army days he designed posters and had his own wee pad which was the envy of his mates as you can imagine. He is now the owner of a sketch book and his first picture is of a cat with pyjamas which looks very recognisable but drawing is not my subject so anything would look good to me. The very fact that he used the book was a bonus to me. For those who do not know there is a saying "The Cats Pyjamas" which means in high regard and he says that is how he feels about the sketch book. Eureka! I hope that there will be many more enlightened drawings somewhere in his brain and who knows maybe a form of communication also. Nothing can be ruled out!! Keeping George occupied helps his moods so the drawing can be rubbish as long as he enjoys doing them.

2nd December 2013

George is in hospital again with a rapid heart beat which was probably caused by a urinary tract infection which he has had in the past and his heart seems to be alright. The Physio is assessing him with a view to getting back home as he is very unsteady on his feet. He has had an eye on my indoor walking frame with the tray for some time as it does make walking much easier so 'Yes' we have ordered another one for him and I have now lost count of the walking aids in this house. Traffic lights will be the next requirement!!!! I am keen to keep George on his feet as it would be a different ball game if he could no longer walk and we would need a lot more help which I want to avoid as long as possible as it encroaches on your privacy but may be necessary in time. We now have a stair lift installed which is proving to be more helpful than I thought it would be and I have become rather attached to it as it is so useful for getting up the stairs with washing and all the other stuff having to be moved around. It is not the speediest of contraptions and meanders up our large stair well very sedately but truth be told it is quite relaxing and no sore legs at the top. George uses it but needs a helping hand. HOW LIFE CHANGES. At one time long ago I could jump the last three stairs into the hall and land safely. Douglas boasted that he could jump five stairs but that was just his big head!

8th December 2013

George is now back home again from hospital and another spell of being well looked after by the NHS. He had a urinary tract infection and slight chest infection which have cleared up. Bloods, heart and liver are all in good working order so not too bad for a 90 year old. His blood pressure is even normal without loads of pills. With a memory that works life would be perfect but who promises 'perfection'. Many younger people to-day would not pass a liver test and the sad bit is that they do not listen. What's changed?
It is now becoming necessary for George to have help putting cream on and getting to bed at night although he does not think so. However it is becoming more demanding for me when problems arise at bedtime and even the hospital were

surprised that he did not have help at night. I am inclined to put off more help as long as possible as it does disrupt our home life but I now know the benefits of having carers dress him in the morning   so it will be an extension of this and he is very happy with the attention he gets in the morning.

He attends a club on a Wednesday with Antoinette now and has fitted in fairly well but says they are all old people (he is not of course). It seems that there was only one man at this club so they were keen to get a companion for him. Unlike George he is an extrovert type and enjoys taking the floor dancing and singing but George is happy to watch and he is allowed to do this which makes it more relaxing for him..

Christmas has arrived and on Christmas Eve Sheila took us to her house where she has her annual come as you go for her friends. I took George this year because he does not like being alone. He stayed for five hours which was longer than I thought was possible. Sometimes I think that we should now stay at home at Christmas as to me George strikes a lonely figure sitting quietly with fun going on around him. The same applies to Christmas day which Lesley and Iain arrange so well but George has very little part of it and again I know that he would rather be at home. I I like going out so George gets no option really. My feelings are mixed about the arrangements because it saddens me to see him in his own wee world with all the festivities going on and It suits me to have him with us but I am certain that if George had the ability to decide for himself he would have different ideas. Next year if we are still around I see changes and may just leave the family to get on with things. Dementia cannot be switched on and off and the person afflicted by it must be considered. I am aware of Sheila and Lesley also who have to transport us from A to B when it is a busy time for them and the last thing I want is to be a millstone round their neck. It is no big deal at our age when we have happy memories of previous Christmases.

Ben, Linda and Layla had Christmas dinner with us at Lesley's and I enjoyed their company especially seeing Layla and how grown up she is becoming, a smashing wee girl. Again George had no idea of who they all were and is completely confused by them and asked endless questions about who they were and of course forgot what he was told almost immediately which makes me wonder why the so called experts say it stimulates the mind to have them in company. Not true he just likes his own chair in his own house I am sure of that. I will admit that he enjoys the one to one company of his befrienders and the wee social he goes to each Wednesday with them with people his own age group who have time to listen to him. He is more animated when he comes home from those outings than any other thing he does. The exception here is the Christmas lights that Sheila took us to see and he still talks about them after two weeks.

Because I am writing this story I can bore you with our Christmases seventy years ago. We worked as normal on Christmas day then went home to chicken and mince pies made by mum, no alcohol available. From there we either went dancing or to one of the many cinemas showing exotic American Movies. On New Year we had one day off and Hogmanay was my mum's time when the Whisky and Sherry came out of the sideboard and she dusted the house from top to bottom before first footers came in. Ginger Wine was my drink. We usually went dancing on Hogmanay and first footed my parents then bed by 1 am. It may seem tame but my memories are all happy. It never fails to sadden me to see the amount of drink consumed today and especially the very young, who treat it as normal. It seems that they have a lack of belief in themselves but there will sure be a price to pay eventually. We did have our drunks seventy years ago but usually in the older age bracket and most families had a member who over indulged. There was a lot less money and also alcohol was less readily available. Supermarkets had not come in to our environment and in my opinion they have a lot to answer to for the availability of alcohol and their cut price approach making it too easy to come by. Surely the powers that be will knock their heads together some day and sort out at least underage drinkers. While on the subject I enjoy my glass of wine so I am not against drinking as such. This is now the 1st January 2014 and we had a quiet New Year as was expected, I did not even have a drink as I was on my own George being in bed.

George was a bit under the weather a few days ago with a slight cough and hoarse so because of his past history of landing in hospital I phoned the doctor late in the afternoon for advice. Being the good GP that he is he said he would come in on his way home which was 6.30pm. The pills that George was prescribed were very large and he had difficulty swallowing them so the next day late in the afternoon again I phoned the doctor .This was Hogmanay and no doubt they were anxious to get home but the GP phoned my chemist just before he closed to get medicine in liquid form and to put the icing on the cake as it were the chemist had them delivered to me by an assistant who lives are still many good and caring people in the world.

I had a visit from John Kelly, his two daughters and his partner a few days ago when George was on one of his afternoon trips. We had a nice afternoon as I had not seen his daughters for some years and they are now young ladies. George appeared home early and arrived home to a house full of people he did not recognise. I reminded him that John was his late cousin Archie's son so he seemed to accept it. However when they left he changed completely and said that they had come to visit because they wanted our money. No amount of talking convinced him that it was a friendly visit and I got quite angry because I had such a lovely afternoon. I am not going to dwell on this episode as it is all part of a horrible illness but I was distressed and thanks to Sheila calmed down slightly and changed my mind about putting him in a Home (only a temporary blip) It happened before with Anne and Subi when they visited and he thought they were here to buy our house.

19th January2014   George has had two falls recently and on the last one when he fell between his bed and the window managed to crack a rib. I had to call the emergency service which I am connected to and they lifted him off the floor but the second time at 11pm Sheila and Lesley were there before them as they were on call to someone else who had fallen. They got him into bed and he seemed fairly good. Lesley however decided to stay the night with me in case of further developments. This being the weekend we could not phone our GP till Monday when George was having pain in his ribs. Our great GP called in and left Co-Codomol which I soon found that the pills were too large for him to swallow and as they were capsules could not be halved. Phoned GP again (Hogmanay by this time) .It was late afternoon but doctor phoned chemist to get liquid medicine for him which was delivered to our door at 6.30pm by staff at chemist. Nothing wrong with the NHS!!!

Unfortunately the Co-Codamol did not agree with him and he felt quite ill so phoned GP again and back he came to see George to sort things out.

I was beginning to realise that I could no longer continue without more help as I did not want to run Sheila and Lesley into the ground. Having carers and others into your house can be invasive but if George was to remain at home something had to be done and I know that our doctor felt the same as he was also concerned about me. So Helen at Social Work again to see if he could get back in to Munro Court Care Centre twice a week once more. It seems that they have a place and I am having a visit next week to discuss this. Thanks to Lesley and the grapevine at Yorkhill Hospital plus Face Book I now have two different lovely ladies who stay overnight and take the pressure off me by giving me a good night's sleep. The plus side is that we only pay £40 per night compared to nearly £100 charged by the large combines. Even the doctor was amazed that we were paying so little and his concern was that they were up to it. I assured him that they were well vetted by Lesley and her colleagues.

I now have carers in the morning, carers at night to prepare him for bed, a sleepover lady and his various outings during the week. Never in my wildest dreams would I have thought I could have had all this change in our lives but so be it if George can stay at home for longer. At one stage in our long journey of Dementia I felt isolated and alone sometimes but not now as the carers take time to chat so we have a bit of a laugh sometimes. It proves that human nature can deal with change when we have to.

All the work I have with George seems nothing when I think back to my Mum's day being reared in the Gorbals in a room and kitchen house with only her mum to care for her and her two siblings. My Gran made time to support the Suffragette Movement and worked long hours to feed her family. My own mum's dedication trying to make the world a better place for working class people knew no bounds and she had loads of 'causes' she fought for so I wonder what she would think of living conditions in 2013. I do not remember her speaking of Food Banks or such but she did speak of the warm hearted neighbours around them. I do not see much of that dedication to-day but maybe there is somewhere. Improvements have been made in many ways but I suppose if Mum came back she would still find a 'cause' to fight for. I just feel grateful for the help that is around to-day but sometimes it is hard tracking it down. With council cut backs the time carers stay with George has been cut and they are expected to get him out of bed, washed and creamed over his whole body then dressed all in quarter of an hour which is impossible. With a patient like George he is slow but this is not taken into account and by the time he is sitting down for breakfast he more often than not lets out a huge sigh which shows the effect it has on him never mind the carers. It unsettles me at times that George has to be so hurried in the morning but no answer here.

I said further back in my story that George would not go back to Munro Court Care Home as he felt happier at home. Never say never George is now back in Munro Court on a Tuesday and Friday as I was feeling the strain having to be more watchful since his falls. He has had his first week and seems to have settled, he even won the Bingo first day there so that pleased him. There is no way he could stay at home without all this help so no more to be said about it.

With the help of Social Workers and especially our GP life is much more positive now and I am grateful to them all but to a large extent Sheila and Lesley have been so helpful and always on call when they are needed. We keep a light on for George at night now as his first fall seemed to be because he was disorientated in the dark and he probably forgot where the light switch was.

Lorraine my favourite overnight angel comes twice a week now and for the remainder of the week at the moment I cope well but I am fully aware that circumstances can change rapidly so we have a small list of overnighters to call on if necessary keeping life as normal as possible.

Some very good carers from Cordia attend to George morning and night and they work a week on and a week off. One such carer is Cathie who at the moment is replacing Senga our past carer who is off long term with a shoulder injury. Cathie is working her week off at no extra money as staff is in short supply but she loves her work and it shows. Her dedication is genuine and she always has a smile and kind word. They all bring their own persona to the job, some give hugs and some are a laugh a minute, others do their job and go. How lucky we are and to think that I once doubted them.

George is accepting Munro Court Day Centre but the hour before he is picked up is demanding answering endless questions as to where he is going as he does not remember having been there before. Getting his outdoor clothing on is a nightmare as he wears so many clothes (and is still cold). Going to the toilet takes up a lot of his time also as he forgets he has been. I am ready to drop by the time he eventually walks out the door and it is only 10am. Munro Court was set up to support me with the backing of many others so with that in mind I will look forward now to relaxing to Strauss Waltzes by the Vienna Philharmonic Orchestra and maybe a cup of coffee.

According to George Musical Chairs was the order of the day at Munro Court but remembering them from my younger days I cannot imagine the scene trying to grab the last chair. I just could not picture George and his walking aid rushing around so I was pleased to be told that he decided to sit out for this one. I have since been told that there is a modified version of the game which is a relief as A&E would not appreciate it. I'm told that George has a lady friend, twenty years his junior, who rushes to help him when he arrives at the Garthalmock Social Club which he attends every Wednesday. She recently lost her husband so has obviously adopted George as a surrogate. There is no need to become perturbed as he forgets her from one week to the next. He seems to have settled down at the Club and maybe I know the reason now!!! His mind is usually filled with the seated

222

exercises he does with the help of a Video but he told me there were only two men and about eighteen women at Munro Court so I asked him if he fancied any of them but his answer was that my figure is better than any of theirs (his eyesight is dodgy). Also that some of the women had peroxide hair out of a bottle so his powers of observation are good, at least for the females. He also knows what side his bread is buttered and not to ruffle my feathers or else..............

It is well in to February now and had another 'can't cope' episode recently but a tearful chat with Lesley sorted things out for the present. George is not always to blame as we all have bad days but when it happens to me everything becomes more stressful and difficult. His lack of hearing is a big problem as he becomes downcast when the hearing aids are not functioning properly.

Residential care is on my mind now but my ambition is to keep him at home for the summer months if I can as he loved his Gazebo last year so it would be nice to let him have another year of it and Sheila and Lesley agree so with the help available this may be a realistic plan but only time will tell.

One positive side recently has been that with the help of a very special carer who comes in about 8.30 at night to prepare George for bed and has persuaded him to retire to bed at that time thus giving me time on my own and not having the hassle of seeing him to bed at 10.30 when he once went. Those small things make such a difference and as long as he has his microwavable teddy with him he seems quite happy and in no time at all is fast asleep.

27th February 2014

There is not a lot to report about George at the moment and he is still going to bed about 8.30pm. It has become routine now which is good for me. Each day brings one problem or another to surmount as his condition slips downhill a bit but he has clear moments which are welcome and are forgotten just as quickly by him. He is noticeably more forgetful and much less able to deal with problems resulting in him getting angry with himself. Now that the weather is improving and light nights are approaching he has this urge to go a walk with his rollator and it is hard to explain to him that it is not possible as he is so unsteady on his feet. Walking round the garden is not an option for him as he has been a keen walker all his life as we always owned dogs. However he will have to be content with the garden this summer and no doubt will accept it in time. My commitment to having him at home as long as possible and especially during the coming summer months wavers at times. Some days are more demanding than others which is partly because I am not in top form every day and it usually coincides with him being more difficult also.

There can be good occasions too as when he was at the Social Club one Wednesday with Jacqui and said that he was the only man among about twenty women (they say women live longer than men but George disproves this) I asked him if he fancied any of them but he was very tactful (he knows who to keep in with) and said that none of them had a figure like mine and some were blondes out of a bottle but George has dodgy eyes so I must make allowances and not get too big headed. Is it possible that George sees me as the teenager he first met?

It is unsettling coming to the decision to put a lifelong partner into Residential Care and also to decide when the correct time to do this. I feel he has as much right to live at home in the house he knows as I have but his memory problems put him in a more uncertain predicament as he cannot make decisions for himself which puts those looking after him in a vulnerable position.

George has a place at Munro Court on a Monday now so that is three days per week and a day at the Social Club with all the ladies. Also every second Thursday at the Glenkirk Centre which has been on the go for some time now.

I have more time to myself but as human nature would have it I am taking time to adapt to an empty house. I will really have to try and get my social life or what is left of it on track but it is not easy due to the fact that I cannot walk far so it looks like the scooter will have to be conquered when summer comes. I appreciate time on my own to get my head sorted out so I cannot have it both ways. According to those who look after George at the Care Home he seems to have settled in well and takes part in some activities, others he sits out which is fine as he always did his own thing in his younger days. I feel sad when I see George going off to Munro Court as I am conscious that he would rather sit in his chair looking out his large window, which he installed and that this is being done for my benefit alone but maybe it is the only way to stay sane.

I think we will deviate a bit now and hope whoever reads this is interested in my memories of the year that George and I got married which was 1949. We had come from a generation that had seen many scientific discoveries the most horrific being the atom bomb in 1946 but thankfully now used for more peaceful purposes. In 1949 we would have been laughed off the face of the earth at the idea of a woman carrying a personal telephone in her handbag or chatting to all and sundry while walking along the street. The large black phone was just putting in an appearance for us ordinary people but it was nearer 1960 when George and I acquired one in the first house we bought. We discussed in depth whether we could afford to keep it as we had just taken on our first mortgage so every penny was important. We decided as it was already installed we would keep it much to my delight. At this time telephone lines were in short supply as all lines were overhead so we shared a line with another family which could be annoying if you wanted to make a call and they were already on the phone. It was possible to hear their conversation if you so wanted but they heard a click when the other party tried to get on the line and you knew that they could be listening. We were glad when eventually our own private line was installed. Who could have perceived that in 2014 I would own two mobile phones and two land line ones as well as a computer and a television that works almost like a computer or so it seems to me. Letter writing was also more frequent in 1949 and to me much more personal than texts as they could be kept and re-read umpteen times. I still have the first letter that George wrote to me in the 1940s and it is still as fresh looking today as the day he wrote it. Letters written one day would always be delivered next day so it was possible to meet someone at fairly short notice. Letter writing was also important to George and I during the time he served in the forces for three years and it was the only communication we had. The younger generation will not agree with me but a text can never be as personal as a letter. The many letters found eighty years later by soldiers serving in the First World War are testimony to this and have historical significance. Who will eve r find a text eighty years from now?

While I am straying off course and remembering how life 'once was' and the 'progress' we have made during that time, we had a wind up gramophone someone gave us which I thought was incredible even though you had to keep winding this thing or the music stopped. I say Music but it sounded really screechy and awful. Given that our home in Bilsland Drive had no gadgets at all, not even a potato peeler, having a gramophone was ace. There was no electricity hence the need for wind up contraptions. Our house was lit by gas lamps which used a mantle which broke when you breathed on them so had to be constantly replaced. We did have an inside loo and bath but no wash basin, the kitchen sink being good enough. All cleaning was done by pure hard graft and tough women.

There was a large chimney in this house with a ledge just inside it which my dad hid prezzies, usually sweets. We had to call up for whatever we wanted and hey presto it appeared and I believed it all. Needless to say the fire would not be lit when this happened. Happy days!!!!!

Electricity appeared in our lives when we moved to Scotstounhill to an upstairs downstairs new house. My brother was upstairs switching on the stair light and I was downstairs putting it off which to us was sheer magic. Life was so uncomplicated in the 1930s before I pads and such like surfaced.

Now to return to the wonderful world of 2014 and believe me I know that there is a lot to be thankful for living in this era not least the great progress in medicine and people living longer but good genes are a key factor in how long we live. When taking a trip down memory lane we have to be mindful that our memory can play tricks and sometimes we only remember the good bits and forget the bad episodes which in some ways is fortunate.

7th March 2014

This has not been one of the best weeks culminating with George being at his most difficult to-day Friday and waiting to be picked up for Munro Court and also I am rubbish in the morning as I have said before. His memory does not let him remember having been at Munro Court before even though he goes three times a week so it worries him and he constantly asks about it and says he wishes he knew where he is going. It can be very exhausting but all part of this long haul to keep George at home as long as possible.

George had a wee accident at the social club on Wednesday and he was mortified that they had to give him a change of underwear. Although he is fairly continent for now I decided to try him with Tena pants and they have given him so much more confidence. I did not realise how much it had been worrying him and thought he may refuse to wear them but the opposite has been the case. This is a personal dilemma for George but unfortunately all part of dementia thus part of the story.

In a follow up from the previous paragraph, my GP once informed me that the surgery had an incontinence nurse who would be pleased to discuss problems at any time. I had a picture in my mind of this wee nurse sitting waiting for me to call and help me get a free supply of incontinence aids so a call to the surgery but as would have it she was out so left my phone number. A call next morning from Nurse at 8am did not start my day well. However she at least phoned back but left me another number to phone. A quick look around for pencil and paper at my bed and I noted the number which was good-bye to surgery nurse and the thought that she was waiting there for me to phone at any time. When I had wakened up a few hours later I phoned the number but was then given another number and despatched to this electronic female who proceeded in her squeaky voice to give me all the options for incontinence. This verbal onslaught went on for a while till she finally said that if I was a new patient I was to get in touch with my GP. I had gone full circle so to save my sanity decided it was easier to pay for the goods. Sheila however has taken up the challenge and disappeared with my note and all the phone numbers so good luck Sheila. I wonder why the people responsible for our services make it all sound so easy when they are first contacted and give us a false sense of security. Believe me few things are easy when help is needed.

Now that George is settled with Care Home and Social Club on week days I have more time for myself and certainly less stress. It has made a sizeable change to my life and since our retirement did more together. Until my mobility went downhill a few years ago we walked the dog going round all the Glasgow parks and down the coast for a breath of fresh air but we still had our own pastimes and activities.

It is an inevitable part of life that the older you become mobility is an issue and George has also dementia to contend with. Because my legs will not do as I ask them I am confined to the house more than I would like and when George is away the house seems empty after a life time of always being in company either at home or work. In the past I longed for just this situation when balancing family, work and elderly parents. I'll give you a wee quote here "By the time you are old enough to know your way around, you're not going anywhere"

I have to tackle the reality that after 65 years we are no longer a 'twosome' and George is in his own world forgetting the past while I still remember. Maybe another way of looking at the situation is that we have had so many years in not bad health be it luck or genes. Given time I will find my feet and enjoy the freedom. That last sentence is a bit of a pun my walking being what it is but it just came out so I will leave it there.

14th March 2013

George had another nasty fall in the bathroom at 1am a few nights ago and I was awakened by an almighty crash as he went down hitting his back on the edge of the shower as he fell, I dialled 999 and the response guy came in ten minutes or thereabouts followed by an ambulance which happened to be in the area at the time so we had loads of help. I also had the brass neck to phone Lesley at such an unearthly hour but felt I needed support in case he went to hospital. Poor George was surrounded by so many people he was completely bemused. The decision was that he did not require hospital treatment and was put back in bed. The extremely nice emergency team went on their way leaving us knackered so Lesley kindly stayed for the remainder of the night but we did not sleep well as you can imagine.

We now have a bucket in his room to avoid him going to the bathroom during the night which he thought was rather unhygienic at first and we also removed any furniture he might hit if he fell. This, with the aid of lighting seems to be working but I find it hard to sleep well.

I now know that the time has come for George to be looked after in a care home as I find it impossible to sleep soundly at night and he cannot keep having falls or he will seriously injure himself eventually.

I thought it wise to try and prepare George for the fact that he could be going in to fulltime care. I knew this would not be easy because of his hearing and memory problems so had to wait for the right time if there ever is one. At the beginning he was horrified and said he would kill himself if that happened but after a bit of explaining he settled down slightly and listened to what I had to say. I assured him that it would not happen immediately and he was relieved and told me he would have to get his head round it which I thought was rather positive. His big worry was how I would manage on my own which I thought was nice. As we continued our conversation at a slow pace, memories came back to him of Rennie, his sister's husband and a neighbour once being in

Erskine Home at Anniesland and us visiting them there. It took me by surprise that he remembered because he could never summon up any memories before of Rennie. This was good news as he thought it was a nice place when he visited. Proof of having served in the armed forces is a qualification to gain entry to Erskine Home. George served in the Royal Corp of Signals during the war so more good news. Now to start enquiries about George gaining entry so Social workers have to become involved and this is a very slow process along with funding and all the other hoops to jump through. Events unfortunately overtook us as George was admitted to Gartnavel Hospital with a chest and urinary infection. His back where he fell was also very painful and he could not walk. My worst nightmares of George going to hospital had come true and on my first visit nothing changed my mind. Parking was madness so Lesley dropped me off at the door and I made my way to Ward 3c to be confronted by about 50 people all waiting for the one lift that seemed to be in working order. Crowds and lifts do nothing for me but I had to see George so be stoic and wait for lift as there was no way I could walk upstairs. I arrived at the ward to be confronted by what seemed like chaos with trolleys with distressed patients in them and just a very busy scene. I got through to George who was in a single room which was good and as Lesley approached I burst into tears and said I was taking him home. From the chaos two nurses appeared and assured me that he would be fine and offered me a cup of tea (which never came) Something stronger was more essential at this point, even sedation. One Flew Over the Cuckoo's Nest came to mind but I obviously came at a bad time as in the two weeks he was there it was calmer although as is expected in the NHS now a shortage of nurses and George got the basics but was bored out of his mind alone in that sterile room. If we had not visited every day he would have been in a worse state. With his memory it was hard to explain that we would be back the following day so we tried writing things down but doubt if he read the notes. George is always well liked by the staff in hospitals because he does not give them any trouble and thanks them profusely when they attend him but sometimes it pays to do a bit of shouting and get noticed!

George is now in a Care Home at Maryhill which is a vast improvement from where he came from. He has his own room with Television and can see out his window to some sort of gardens. This is temporary until a permanent place can be found and Erskine at Anniesland had no vacancies at the moment so we are looking around very carefully as we want this move to be the final one. Social Work are still on his case regarding funding and all the rest of the stuff associated with the move. It is not an easy time for any of us at the moment and I have had big adjustments myself living alone for the first time in my life but just another obstacle to overcome.

We are surprised at how well George has settled in at "4 Hills Care Home" and he seems to have forgotten about his home at Eastcote Avenue which is good as far as he is concerned. This Care Home is only a temporary arrangement until a permanent place can be found so it means he will have another move which will not go down well with him but we will cross that bridge later. We found a small Care Home in

Anniesland Road but it had to be ruled out as it did not do nursing care which George requires due to his falls and urine infections so we are now pushing Erskine House at Anniesland and we once again have Brenda on our side as she has some connections with Erskine (Brenda is the partner of Cameron's dad) She helped once before when George sliced his thumb on a circular saw by using her influence at the plastic surgery unit in the Royal Infirmary. In this fraught business of finding the best place for George we have learned that the more people pushing the sooner we hope to have a solution to the problem.

Meanwhile at the moment I am converting our back sitting room into a bed sitting room for myself as it is downstairs and nearer the kitchen should I wish to make a cup of tea. There is also a toilet handy so my wee 'flat' will be complete when I take delivery of a few bits of furniture. It is a large room with patio doors to the rear garden. I am still not convinced that it will work as I like my room upstairs but I can always go back if I am not happy.
One night spent in my wee flat convinced me that I preferred to sleep upstairs which I felt sure would happen. However the downstairs room is a lovely second sitting room and the bed is always there should I require it in the future.. We have been fifty years in this house so this must prove how I hate 'change' Even moving downstairs in the same house was too much for me!!!!

April 2014

The last four weeks I have gone from 'overload' to practically zero, George being in a Care Home, no carers are coming around the house or people to take him out but three cheers no Social Worker (sorry Helen). It is very lonely and quiet but I use my radio more and enjoy some programmes that I did not know existed. Five years looking after George has been a roller coaster but one that I had to do and would do again if necessary. If the position was reversed and I was the one who was ill George would have done the same for me. I only realise now how wearing the past two years have been now that it has stopped. George will spend his remaining years in residential care and whether he moves to Erskine at Anniesland is not in our hands as he has to wait for a place to come up. Also we would have to seriously consider his position at Four Hills as he says he is happy there and we want the best for him.

Our long retirement so far has been free of money worries and a lot of credit must go to George as through our married life, and before, he studied at various colleges and Universities doing degrees in his special subject in teaching which was Production Engineering and latterly Management Services. He studied into middle age along with full time employment at Stow College, three children and a dog at home. I take credit here as I kept things together at home while he was doing this but it paid off as he reached the top of his career thus giving us an easier life financially. George gained satisfaction from teaching and was highly thought of by lots of his students who did well in their studies. It seems weird that he now requires a memory board to know the day of the week and also who visited him that day. He never fails to thank us for visiting which is certainly not necessary. My story of George and I living with dementia has ended as I no longer look after him and he now has round the clock professional care and I hope no more falls. The high point was reached this week (6th May 2014) when I was visiting and we were chatting about Four Hills. He said that he was very happy to be there and would never like to come home again. This could have been offensive perhaps but not to me as I was so pleased that he had settled enough to feel this way. He has no memories of his home at Eastcote Avenue at all and it is all just part of this illness but it does not worry him so cheers for that! He has no problem recognising Sheila, Lesley and myself which is good and always asks if we will be back the following day and we will continue this for as long as it takes making sure he is taken care of appropriately. I knew this would not be the end so I must tell you about an incident that happened yesterday at Four Hills to prove how perceptive George's mind still is. He was at Lunch and the man opposite him leaned forward in his chair but George knew that he was not checking what he had on his plate. He was actually 'blowing off' on the QT. According to the staff at Four Hills they are convinced that George does lip reading so we can now add body language to his talents now. He is probably guilty of this himself and that is why he knows so much about it.

To-day (11th May)   Lesley and I were sitting with George at the Dining Room where the residents were waiting for their Evening Meal. It takes almost an hour to get them seated for a meal as they are in various stages of Zimmers. George suddenly said he thought he saw a mouse or maybe a rat as it was quite big I lifted my legs pronto off the floor but it was a wee dog he had seen through t glass doors. We dreaded to think what devastation he would have caused had the residents in the Dining Room heard him…

21st May 2014

Don't know why I thought that George going in to full time care would end my story as wee anecdotes still occur that may or may not interest anyone spending their time reading this.

When we visit George now at Four Hills we have to look for him as he no longer sits in his room afraid to move. How is that for progress? Gone are the days at Gartnavel when he was scared to leave his room because of a reprimand from Staff. Being summer we now know that he will be sitting somewhere in the sun. Four Hills has lots of small private sitting areas dotted around which are highly inviting to sit in and we always took George from his room to sit in one of those areas so he is now going on his own which is progress indeed. The head nurse tells us that he walks about quite freely now which is further proof he is settled and happy. After visiting George today Sheila and I went to Dobbie's for some plants for our gardens. We came along Bilsland Drive and turned into Balmore Road and I know that Sheila does not realise how nostalgic this route is to me retracing my steps of early childhood and spending time with a chum in Balmore Road. I wonder if those memories become more vivid as we get older or maybe just more time to think about them. That was also the route we took on the motor bike to land in on Granny Hunter in Torrance and it is amazing how little it has changed apart from the occasional round-about and of course more traffic.

It is now June, summer being the season I like best but mega differences this year as I am now on my own for the first time in my long life. George has been out of his house for three months now and has absolutely no memories of it so we know he is not pining for his old haunts and seems very happy where he is. I cannot imagine a life without memories as mine are very treasured and I can look back on them in a nice way.

The last three months have been uphill for me suddenly being alone and at first there was a sense of relief in some ways that I could relax and only think about myself and not feel on edge most of the time but that has passed on to another phase and I feel less positive now and know that this situation is for all time. The benefits help me to overcome those feelings such as the evening meal is so much easier and I can enjoy my food now without interruptions also I see George most days so that fills a gap. There are many reasons to be grateful so life will go on. George also praises the food at Four Hills and it looks very appetising and all cooked on the premises. Plenty cups of tea supplied throughout the day as well so there are always things to be happy about if we look for them.

This next wee anecdote concerns a letter I received from George when I was sixteen asking me on a date to the Cinema. I had known him a short time through the Albert Ballroom and a 'foursome' we had with my friend Margaret and George's cousin Archie who was a handsome six footer and Margaret fancied him a lot. George had recently finished a relationship with a girlfriend in my favour it seems so hence the letter.

The outcome of this was that Lesley posted the envelope with the date, 15th October 1942 and the head of King George on the stamp on Face Book. It got some lovely comments and even a photograph of our old house in Danes Drive from a friend of my granddaughter Lucy who now lives directly across the road. Sometimes Face Book can be drivel but it also has its moments and this was one of them and the reaction it caused. To most of the generation who responded I suppose a handwritten letter is weird especially one 72 years old but how many texts will be around in seventy years? A handwritten letter is so much more special than any amount of texts or Emails and this one is still unique to me after all those years. Sad to say it does not summon up any memories to George now. Looking on the bright side he does ask where I am and if I am alright if I miss a visit so we'll settle for that.

June 13th 2014   Speaking to George I become baffled with this memory business and how it works or in his case sometimes fails to work. His birthday is approaching and I asked him today what date he was born and he immediately said 3.7.23 which is correct. I pushed him further and asked him if he remembered his army number but he did not so I told him that I remembered it and he replied that I had written lots of letters to him so naturally I would remember it which I thought was smart of him being able to work that out. Being on a roll I asked him if he remembered my address he wrote to in reply and he quickly said 264 Danes Drive which was also correct. He also recalled 46 Foxbar Drive where he lived in Knightswood at one time. When it came to our house in Eastcote Avenue that we have lived in for fifty years and he only left three months ago he had no recall. The memory must have many pockets where experiences are stored and we try to find a trigger to find them when talking to George. This can be demanding with his lack of hearing but worth it to see the joy on his face when it is successful. Surely the medical profession will soon be able to find the answer to this frustrating illness.

Throughout my life (Nancy's turn now) I have always been attached to some group or other dancing as a child and singing in a choir and as I got older amateur dramatics, country dancing, swimming and so on along with bringing up a family. The friendship I acquired from those pursuits was an important part of my life.

Without being too emotional being so limited in mobility now is a big handicap and some people may think well you are 88 so what's your problem? It is a BIG problem because when I am sitting down my brain tells me I can do things but I soon find out that the legs tell another story. To be able to jump on a bus and shop in town is a fond memory now. I visit George most days and he is happy to be looked after which is fine but I am not ready to join him so I will 'stay the course' and try to focus in on what I CAN do still. Being on my own is still a problem but not all of the time, acceptance may come in time. Having companionship all my life it is weird to suddenly be on my own but this was bound to happen to one or other of us eventually. I take exception to some acquaintances who tell me how well I am coping. How

do they know? Each day is different and has challenges and I am the only one who knows if I am coping. My diversions are the Radio which I have rediscovered and of course writing this stuff. A few days ago my neighbour Mavis came up the garden path and gave me a big bear hug and asked how things were and how George was getting on. We are good neighbours
going a long way back but do not see each other much. However on that day she knew how to make me feel better.
19th June and Sheila took George and I to Canal Banks at Kilsyth where there are lots of boats and Ice Cream which was appreciated on such a warm day. George is never keen to leave his Nursing Home into the outside world now probably because he is well established in Care Home routine but we felt that a spell away from his routine would be beneficial. He did refuse to get out of the car which was fine with us at least he was out in the big world.

Being a sunny day there was lots of bare skin around some not very pleasant and the bold George became fixated on this to such an extent that he began counting the number of men with no vests on and how awful some of them looked. Those beautiful canal locks we had taken George to and all he could see was bare skin. I think the next time we take him a run on a nice day we will just go around the streets of Drumchapel and really make his day or maybe even nearer to Partick.

I am at the moment getting over a bout of Gout on a finger which is extremely painful and also at the same time a painful heel which is impossible to walk on so this with all the other annoyances is demoralizing . I missed two days visiting George and sat at home in my misery. During that time I had a phone call from Belinda the boss at Four Hills saying that George was very upset as he had got into his head that I was dead and with a telephone enhancer I managed to speak to him and assure him that I was still in the land of the living. It was hard convincing him when I really felt 'rubbish'. It worked out well and he soon forgot about my 'death'

He complains about being lonely just now and it is hard because there is little he can do to pass his time. Belinda has given him a large jig saw which has worked slightly although he finds it difficult with co-ordination but the plus side is that some of the carers come in as they are passing his room and place in a few pieces to help him along. This I hope has the double effect of having contact with people coming into his room and helping his loneliness. Sheila is now on holiday from school so this helps. His 91st birthday is on 3rd July which is this week so we will take him a run and I believe the chef bakes a cake for birthdays but we have warned them to play it down as he does not like a fuss so they understand. 2nd July This week has not been good for George as his brain is not functioning well and added to that he has swollen legs which are also itchy. Today he has to stay in his room with feet elevated and cream three times a day on legs. He is also on more tablets to try and stop the itch which I feel are making him do'lally(Belinda's word). However it is a vicious circle as he needs the tablets to give him some peace. All in all today was difficult with his change of routine being confined to his room. Any change in routine for dementia

sufferers is hard for them and this small change threw
George completely today and it took Sheila more than an
hour to get through to him what it was all about and that his
legs would get better if he rested. I am still struggling with
my gout and sore heel so I just left Sheila to talk George
round. She was convinced he would understand in time as
this sort of situation has arisen before when he convinced
himself that I was selling the house. He eventually said that
he understood what was going on now much to our relief and
that he was glad we came which made it all worth while. We
left him with his Haggis and Neeps sitting in his chair in the
room and his parting shot was 'I love you' A 'draining'
experience. Birthday day tomorrow and lets hope he is
feeling better. We were going to take him a run but not
possible now as he has to elevate his legs which would not be
easy in a car. He does not want a fuss so suits me as we will
just have his usual sherry and cup of tea and keep thin0gs
normal. I have very little use of my right hand at the moment
because of the gout so it takes me four times as long to do the
usual chores but amazing what can be done with one hand.
Just a wee assumption of why my right hand troubles me
with arthritis or gout. In the 1940's and 50's repetitive strain
injury was unheard of we just had a sore hand then. Now it
seems I can give it a name in this great age of discovery. My
thumb, forefinger and middle finger of my right hand are the
fingers with arthritis. In my office job many years ago I spent
long hours writing up ledgers and by the end of the day those
said fingers were quite painful but no thought was given to it
as it was part and parcel of your job. At the very old age of
88 I can now give it an impressive name and maybe blame

Country Dancing and wearing stupid shoes in my teens for the state of my feet now. This is the age of the 'blame' culture so if you can't beat them, join them!!! The trouble is that it changes nothing.

July 14th

Cilla Black at the age of 71 is complaining of going deaf and of course blaming her years in the Cavern for her hearing loss which may be true but it was your choice Cilla and you live with the consequences. Maybe we just need a 'Lorra Lorra' luck to avoid the pitfalls that growing older throws at us instead of looking for someone to blame. There are exceptions such as asbestos which has affected many lives but that is a different story. Otherwise live with the route you choose to take and stop looking for someone to blame if things go wrong. Another 'rant' over!

George has complained about boredom lately so on to the internet and we have come up with various simple games such as animal pairs, quoits and a putting game which have proved very successful and given him something to think about as well as passing the time fruitfully when we visit. It has surprised us how dexterous for his age that George is and they always bring a smile to his face so full marks here. Even Belinda the charge nurse is interested in them for the other residents by asking where we got them. The games must be suitable for players to sit down as we proved when George insisted he stand up when putting and he nearly fell over.

August 2014

August 2014 now …….George is not very well this week
and sleeps a lot and although he likes our visits does not
participate much. His appetite for food has declined also
which is worrying as he usually asks for extras.

We noticed blisters on George's leg and foot which looked
peculiar although they did not seem to be annoying him, but
we hunted down Belinda who is the charge nurse and does
not like any criticism of her department but Lesley and I
were not disturbed by this. She seems to know her job but her
manner leaves a lot to be desired and she can be tactless and
rude at times in an affable way but Lesley has her sussed out
and is equally robust with her in a nice way in order to get
her problems about George sorted out which is our main
concern. Her attitude changed after seeing George's leg and
foot but she assured us that cream was being applied
regularly and hopefully it would settle down. After an
absence of three days holiday we spoke to her again as his
leg was inflamed but she still assured us they were looking
after it but Lesley suggested some tests to be done on it and
also a doctor to see it and this was arranged. She also
appeared with special dressings for his leg which Lesley
approved of and we are awaiting the results of the tests.
Lesley showed a dermatologist in Yorkhill photographs of
the leg and she said it could be an auto immune condition
which would require careful nursing .Sheila and I have been
in to see him each day as she is still on holiday so the staff
know that we are vigilant. Four Hills seems a caring Nursing
Home but when things go wrong a little extra pressure from
the family does not go amiss and keeps them on their toes.
Lesley being a nurse gives added weight.

George has been a resident in Four Hills for five months now and has put down roots better than I would have thought possible, most of his past life has been forgotten and he appreciates our visits each day and always asks when we will be back when we leave him. His brain still works in mysterious ways remembering snippets from the past out of the blue. He has also retained some of his sense of humour but the dark moments are there at times.

Initially when George was taken into full time care there was a certain amount of relief being free of the burden of wakeful nights listening for George getting up for the toilet and the fear of him falling also the constant attention he required at all times. That period passes and is replaced by loneliness and coming to terms with the fact that this situation is for keeps. The long journey of Dementia continues in a different form. Sheila and Lesley are important and dedicate time to visiting and running me around which I give thanks for. This can be very demanding but we try to work things out and not let it take over our lives which I suppose is easier said than done.

As for myself I have to try to find ways of overcoming the empty house syndrome and the bleak spells that occur. I have said in the past that a long walk cures a lot of ills but that is no longer in my agenda. However I have found that it is quite possible to exercise with the aid of a chair and the added help of Abba and I pod. All this in a small way helps the endorphins to get going as much as possible at my age. Movement is so important no matter how small and the biggest effort is getting off that armchair which we become more attached to as the years pass. I fear that the scooter is not in my to-do list so I bought a wee lightweight walking frame which I feel suits me better and the aim here is to walk round the block at least once a day rain or shine. I have also phoned Esther Rantzen's Silverline which puts older people in touch by phone and thus feeling less cut off. I cannot believe that I am writing this but yes it's true but I'll keep an open mind. I think Lesley feels I am looking for a 'fella' but that could not be further from the truth and it is not what Silverline is about. Keep an eye on this space it may be thought provoking or boring……..

14th August 2014
George has developed a chest infection this week which has affected his memory more than is normal so it can be very demanding having conversations with him and also tiring as he worries a lot, probably because he is not feeling in top form so our visiting time is taken up with reassuring him several times that he is on the mend. It must be a difficult time for him as he gets frustrated not remembering things that go on around him and he so appreciates our visits and we hope that we leave him feeling better for our visit. Belinda the charge nurse seemed to be on top of his chest infection as she phoned me to say that he had seen a doctor because she thought he was not so well so full marks there. She makes a point of speaking to us now when we call at Four Hills to assure us that George is being well looked after which we believe is the case. Belinda was inclined to joke about any enquiries we made about George and Lesley always felt she could be more professional so I think we have got through to

her. She always seems caring enough with the patients but our main concern is George and his welfare.

After writing the last paragraph I went to visit George by taxi and Lesley arranged to pick me up at five o'clock. It was obvious he had problems on his mind the minute I walked in to his room. In his confused state he was convinced that he had offended Belinda so I sat down for a long session of cross examination and find out the cause. He could not remember what had happened which is quite usual but he said he would like to say that he was sorry but I could not find the reason so took him out to the sitting area in the hope he would forget. This did not work and he still wanted to say sorry so I hunted out Belinda to get her side of the story. She looked surprised as she often does when confronted with a problem but she came along to see George and assure him that she was not offended about anything. The only thing she could think of was that she had told him to get back into bed that morning as he had not had his medication. She can be rather 'loud' and this may have been the reason for his worries and he does not like confrontation and being the morning was more sensitive. She assured him there was nothing to apologise for and she loved him etc.etc.etc. giving him a few kisses which I don't think he likes. George has difficulty sorting out dreams from reality so we will never know what really goes on in his fuddled brain and can only bring our presence and peace of mind to him.

Today is Sunday August 17th and we decided to take George for a run in the car to try and clear his mind from all his woes so Lesley dressed him in his warm jacket, gloves etc as if we were going to the North Pole and we set off with a cover over his legs also so he was quite happy. You have to remember that George had not been outside for some time as he was never too keen but we felt we had to do something to lift his spirits (or not).

We drove him around the streets he had been brought up in around Knightswood and took the decision to stop at the house he had lived in for 26 years and lo and behold he recognised Foxbar Drive which was a good start. From there we decided to take the risk and pass Eastcote Avenue watching his reaction carefully. Slowing down at our house he remembered it and also Manor Road. Lesley and I had a mixture of emotions when we realised that he had no great feelings for his old haunts and the fact that him and I had shared the house for 50 years and brought our children up in it. To him it just seemed like any other house that he had known. Dementia takes so much away from the person who suffers from it and also those caring for them but we realise that Four Hills is his home now and he is settled there so we are happy with that. Hopefully he returned to the place he knows at Four Hills happier than he was before. The trip he had down memory lane will soon be forgotten unfortunately. George and I live separate lives now which is unavoidable due to his illness and the reality of living on my own is now a fact. It was always something that I was uneasy about as I had never been on my own at any part of my life and I did think about it and wonder if I would be the one left in the house alone as I have been for the last six months. I do not find it easy but I get through it in a kind of a way as we have to and perhaps better than I thought. It has been tough and lonely but my late mum had many quotations and one of them was that if it was always necessary to have a companion then you do not have complete mastery of yourself and that makes me pause for thought (thank you mum!)

She always encouraged me to stand on my own feet but I don't think I was very good at it but those chapters in your life remain with you.

I would not change places with George although he seems happy enough but I still have freedom of choice which he does not. My choices are limited but they are still there and how I get along is up to me and my health of course. Money does not bring happiness but it is one less thing I do not have to worry about and for that I am grateful. Thanks to the part you played in this George. He felt strongly about having enough money in our 'old age' and it is sad that he no longer cares but he would be glad that I benefit from it. The financial side of our marriage has been my responsibility for a number of years now and in the early days George looked after any money we had and I probably spent it but he had a good head for investment and I was happy to let him get on with it. At one time he would have had nightmares about me looking after the cash but I think I am doing alright so George has had more influence on me than I care to think.

9th September 2014

This was a sad day visiting George as he was at a low ebb looking miserable and fed up. The problem is that he cannot remember what has happened to him that day or what is about to happen so he lives entirely in the present moment with no memories of the past or thoughts of the future so it is a lonely place to be. Sheila sat with him and took him through his day from getting up in the morning to going to bed at night. This takes some time and energy because of having to repeat parts due to his hearing loss and inability to focus on what is being said. It helps him momentarily but in no time at all we have to go through it all again as his damaged memory does not hold the reassurances for long. We usually leave him feeling slightly better and he assures us that our visit means a lot to him so we have to settle for the fact that we have made life a bit easier. . It knocks us for six leaving him but we have to realise that we are doing our best and that is all we can do. His mood changes from day to day so we never know what to expect as his brain is constantly working with a clean slate.

George knows that he has two daughters but forgets their names which applies to me also as he thinks my name is Sarah which was his mother's name who has been dead for forty years. He also surprised me one day recently by saying that he thought he may have a son and his name was Douglas who divorced us twenty to thirty years ago and we have not seen him for that time almost. The brain is indeed weird to have recalled that information when he cannot remember what he had for Lunch half an hour ago. He also said that he had no wish to see him so that was a relief as I feel the same. He is someone we knew in a past life and as so much water has passed under the bridge since we saw him we would now have nothing in common with each other (apart from name). I asked George a few days later who Douglas was and he had no idea so that's how it goes.

Another incident happened about this time when he said his outdoor shoes which he has had for two years were not a matching pair and that he wanted the receipt to send them back. One foot was swollen and he could not get it on because of this. He was adamant that the shoes were faulty and wanted a refund. We talked him round but a while later he suggested that we tie the laces together and chuck (his word) them in someone's garden and let them sort it out. This attitude was so unlike him but it made us laugh so a charity shop has now benefitted from them as he only wears special slippers now.

14th November 2014
It is a number of weeks since I have added anything to our story as sadly George died on the 15th October. He had a chest infection, kidney failure and various other conditions. He was well looked after and died very peacefully at 1.40pm with Sheila, Lesley and I with him. Mary, our favourite Nurse was with us and did everything possible to help us through this trying time. We had a private humanist service at Clydebank Crematorium and the family came from far and wide. We plan to scatter his ashes at Rhu a place we visited many times. It has all been kept low key as George would have wanted. A sad time for all of us who were close to George.xxxxxxx
Never in a million years as a sixteen year old when I first met George did I expect to be with him when he died in his 92nd year. It was a long relationship considering my dad said it would never last as I was too young but parents do not always know best. George and Dad turned out to be good

friends eventually. We never regretted our marriage and came through thick and thin as would be expected and I will always feel his loss although he gave us the run-a-round for a number of years before his death with the nasty illness he had but all is forgiven George we learned many things along the way. One significant fact is that he was well liked by all the staff in the Care Home and our GP practice who referred to him as a 'Gentleman' making it so much easier for Sheila, Lesley and myself to look after him even though I have had many moans during demanding times because of his illness.. I would do it all again.

Finally I would like to express my own opinion of Care Homes and their place in society. George was looked after adequately and lovingly but I could see a change in him and something was lost. He was a private person and loved his home so being moved after fifty years in the same house to a place strange to him must have been huge. My wish was to try to keep him at home for the summer months as he loved the warmth and his Gazebo and garden but his health did not allow this. He seemed fairly content at Four Hills but a sparkle had gone from him which could only have been caused by his change in circumstances. He constantly worried about me being left on my own and how I was managing and, of course, if I had enough money which was nice of him.

To remain in familiar surroundings as age catches up with us is so important and my one ambition is to stay out of Care Homes for as long as possible and hopefully for ever. Our marriage was as perfect as can be with disagreements at times but nothing serious. I find it hard to hear couples say that they never argue and I can only imagine one of them must have no brain. George did not like confrontation and was the most forgiving partner so I suppose that leaves me as the obstinate one which I admit to. I will be generous now and forgive him for being the one to split us up and having to spend the remainder of my life without his care and company. Our marriage of sixty five years was not faultless but that would be boring. There is no special formula but having space to follow our own pursuits was important and we did that successfully although we had activities we also shared and probably enjoyed them more because of our independence.

ONLY NANCY

So you thought I had finished well so did I and why I should want to write about myself baffles me but here I am back. 'Only Nancy' was endorsed by Kirsty as she thought it was a suitable title for my next chapter alone. No longer being part of a twosome is hard to learn to live with and caught me unawares but time will sort that out I think but sometimes I think not. Knowing George for seventy years plus and hardly a day without seeing him takes a huge amount of adjusting and is heavy going since George died and I will not deny that it is lonely but I am doing my best to find a way round this. Sheila and Lesley as always call in when they can, I am so glad I have their support which is crucial to me but I have to do my bit as well and maybe that is one of the reasons I am continuing my saga. One of my wee sayings 'You can't look back when you don't look forward' Quite a challenge looking forward at my age.

One thing I must say is that writing stories especially ones that include George have been more helpful to me than I could ever have imagined. There must be something about writing down problems that relieves tension and I am so grateful for my computer as my writing is even more awful now.

Do not get the idea that all was serene and tranquil during our seventy years (maybe at first it was when I was a sixteen year old) It just is not true that there are not tough times in a marriage or partnership but we got through them and looking back we had a happy life and we must have chosen correctly when we were in our teens. My immobility is well recorded, my legs do not work the way I would like but would only take a handful of words to give an account of a day in the life of 'Nancy'. Unless I have to I do not get out of bed until ten o'clock. I had to rise early when George had carers calling on him so maybe this is payback time. It takes longer to wash and dress and do the normal household chores so before I know it two o'clock has arrived and lunch time but only if I feel like it. This is one of the few perks of living alone to eat when hungry. I listen to the Radio a lot and have discovered some interesting programmes and the other kind also but the 'off' switch is handy on those occasions.

Sheila and Lesley call in on a regular basis after work which helps so much. I also have visits from Ishbel and Nan periodically. They are a surviving part of a group of six friends I once had so it is fitting that we live close to each other. Another five friends who were Country Dancing mates

have all departed this world some time ago so I am sort of
Nancy 'no mates' more or less but in saying that the latter
ones were older than me so that figures. Fat chance of me
Country Dancing now anyway!!!! ! So much for Times
Gone By. Now to get on to my exciting life here and now.
For some reason I 'phoned Silver Line a Group started by
Esther Rantzen some time ago for us poor old lonely souls.
They are agreeable enough to chat to which happens weekly
but some of the women come over better than others. Some
would make you yawn with the posh accent and obviously
looking for something in their lives like me. The only
difference is that I am almost housebound and most of them
seem quite young with lives to get on with. Personally I
would rather chat to an older person like myself but I may
get the chance to tell them so. A chat line for older people is
a good thing and I see where they are coming from as some
older people with disabilities who are entirely alone must feel
dreadful so I won't knock it. The one good feeling that
comes from our weekly chats is that I am glad I am not
entirely alone and totally relying on Silver Line. It is all bout
choices and I can still make them.

As time passes we learn to accept the death of someone near
to us although life will never be the same and I am sure that
all of us who were close to George will not forget the
importance he had in our lives. George was mindful that
should I be left on my own I would not be short of cash and
this is one worry I do not have and I never fail to feel grateful
to George and his foresight in our younger days looking into
the future and our retirement years. He worked hard into his
40's improving his qualifications to gain promotion in the job

he loved which was teaching and he reminded me that it was a joint affair between us but he did the hard part I know. He was also a good investor and the lump sum he had at retirement was still invested when he died. Our family have gained hugely by his investments and the good pension he has left.

George had the worry most of his life that he must have plenty cash behind him should we have big repairs to the house. He had to have that 'cushion' His main fear was that the house would require a new roof. We never had any problems with the roof but that made no difference to him. A roofing guy even told us that we had a first class roof and he rarely saw one like ours. He said that he would be out of a job if they were all like ours. Did George believe him? NO…………………………

Recently I have had no less than three Mori polls from Barchester who run Four Hills Care Home for me to take part in a survey and tick boxes telling them how George was being looked after at Four Hills. The fact that he has died does not seem to have passed along the grapevine even after six weeks. It seems that communications in this day and age with all the gimmicks is rubbish so maybe we should go back a bit to talking to each other and stop sending out surveys for dead people to their grieving relatives. Lesley sent Emails to them saying as much and we got the usual apologies but sure enough in the next post another Mori Poll would arrive. It eventually ended with a bouquet of flowers being delivered from Four Hills apologising profusely again. I say it has ended but you never know……. Gillian from Four Hills invited me back when I felt better to see them all (I did have lots of 'friends' among the patients) However I know that this will not happen so thanks but no thanks Gillian – so be it. I have had no less than seven Mori Polls delivered to me asking about Four Hills so they still do not know that George is no longer there. I have already had a bouquet of flowers with apologies so who knows I might get shares in the place yet. The date had passed that the Mori was to be returned so surely that is the end of it now.

This is now the 19th December so Christmas is approaching and although I am looking forward to Christmas at Sheila's this year with the family I will not be sorry when January arrives but in the past I have felt the same so no change there. Nevertheless this year is so different with no George but we will get through it all and come out the other end as we have to. As a token to George, Sheila has had the underfloor heating extended to all her sitting room and Lesley also has new carpets and flooring so upgrading the house a bit. George would have approved of our money being spent on basic items.

Adapting to no longer being a 'couple' takes time and effort but just another 'Everest' to climb. Pointless to say that climbing is totally impossible so scrub the climbing Everest bit. This brings me back to 'thoughts' which do not generate any energy in the legs so plenty potential here.

Sitting comfortably with no ache or pain anywhere because of the fact that I was seated my mind drifts to tasks I could be doing instead of sitting around. After all we are told to keep moving at all costs. The person who invented this theory has obviously no problems with their joints.

Alas once my feet hit the floor t it does not take long to realize that my thoughts had different perceptions from the rest of my body. It would be typical to think I should be familiar with this situation after so many years of poor mobility but the mind does not work that way (at least mine does not) When seated or lying in bed it tells me that I am still capable of doing everyday things like a nice walk or some housework but in reality I often end up making a cup of tea, sitting down with the aim of finding a task in the seated position.

There are times I manage to struggle through jobs urgently needing my attention like woollens to irons because there are none left in my wardrobe and this spurs me on to try more but this rarely happens. The upright jobs need some careful planning with plenty wee rests in between. Believe me what goes on in the head does not travel down to the feet and legs when we have seen too many summers. Somehow the mind seems to think that you are younger and more capable than you are which is hard to make sense of. Surely nature could have synchronized our bodies better. Ironing done and soup made and in the freezer for next week so something achieved. I have just been reading a lovely article in newspaper that people with Spinal Stenosis should not tire themselves too much so three cheers for common sense and I can now relax and do as my body tells me and have no guilt feelings until the powers that be decide we have to exercise again to keep our body mobile.

31st December last day of the year and a phone call from doctor's surgery but not to wish me a Happy New Year. I had a blood test taken recently because of an irritating itch and it seems that the sugar level is slightly high so another one to be taken before eating early in the morning. The weird thing is that in the New Year I had decided to cut down on sweet food a bit. I have taken a liking to Marks & Spencer rich chocolates and I know they cannot be healthy. However the GP beat me to it so I will wait and see the results of next test. Lesley is coming to the house to take the blood at 8am on Monday to save me a visit to the surgery. It is handy having a nurse in the family. No matter what the results I do not plan to buy any more of those nice chocs as I will not push my luck.

I plan to go to bed before midnight tonight as I have done in the past two years because George had no idea that it was New Year so he went to bed at the usual time. Just another day in the calendar. At one time in the very distant past we dance d our way through Hogmanay and the New Year at the Albert Ballroom in Bath Street then first footed my parents but were usually in bed by one o'clock. Happy days!!!

Into January 2015 now and thankful to see the festive season gone but this year more than ever. We had a lovely Christmas dinner at Sheila's this year which we managed to enjoy but thoughts of George were not far away for any of us Coming to terms with the death of someone very close is a solitary situation to be in and I'm sure Sheila and Lesley feel the same but their visits to me are all important and to have no family at all must be awful.

The weather has turned bitterly cold with gales so only ventured out to Marks and Spencer with piles of clothes on. It is the only way I keep in touch with the outside world.

My 'accountant' Sheila and I had a chat to decide what to do with the £72000 invested in a bond with Santander which expires this month. This was a very important 'cushion' for George since he retired and interest rates were high when we took it out but now they are rubbish.

I felt that there was no point in stashing this all away again when interest rates were so low and decided to give Sheila and Lesley £15000 each but buying a new car to replace the Berlingo for Lesley. She was over the moon as this will be the first new car she will have had so happy days there.

It is now the middle of January so the wee bulbs are popping up and nights are getting lighter so can look forward to warmer days.

I have been at the Western Infirmary accompanied by my nurse Lesley to have a Rodent Ulcer removed from my chest. Sounds terrible but I am assured that it will not affect my general health – yahoo! It was scraped out with a spoon like instrument after getting five or so injections so I never felt a thing. Strangely enough the doctor spotted a small cyst on my lip which had been with me for some time so before I knew it this was squeezed out and I was told that it would no longer bother me. I often wonder what it must be like living with skin doctors who notice all those blemishes. Two for the price of one cannot be bad from the NHS.

George was a man of few words but his grandchildren were all important to him and he took them to school and collected them till he was no longer able. He also amused them with a box of tricks he got for a Christmas present one year. In his memory the grandchildren received £250 to put in their bank accounts so they were not forgotten. The remaining £50000 has been invested and will probably go to the family eventually as I am in the fortunate position to have good pensions which will be adequate for my needs. Hopefully it will not be spent on a Care Home for me and that I keep my marbles and just annoy Sheila and Lesley.

3rd March 2015 Not a lot has been happening lately but I have been diverted by writing a wee story about my life at the beginning of our marriage living with my mother-in-law We spent the first ten years of our married life with Sarah my mother-in-law and being newly married it was a happy time tinged with difficult times I found hard to deal with at such a young age but we learn fast and adapt to the situation most of the time or at least we think we do but living with mother in law when newly married is not to be recommended.

My latest purchase for the house is a perching stool for the kitchen. No it is not a parrot but a high stool to enable me to 'perch' when I am working at the kitchen tops thus taking the weight off my legs so no excuses now.

I have also ordered an all round table on wheels which will fit round my armchair and more space for all my rubbish. This sounds a bit more acceptable than the perching stool which involves work in the kitchen.

Being in the house most days I am constantly looking for new pursuits when lack of company overtakes me as perhaps is evident from the last paragraph. You have to remember it takes me some time to do once simple tasks like changing the duvet to-day and having a shower and doing hair which can be exhausting so a cup of coffee and a sit down are necessary after those simple tasks.

When George was at home latterly I had my 'lonely' days also due to his illness and lack of communication so I have had years of experience of this condition. The biggest downside is being unable to up sticks and go out. This is a fact not a moan and I appreciate the faculties I do have. Many articles are written in magazines on how to tackle life when a partner dies by changing your life and getting new interests which is all very well but problematic when your legs won't allow it and very little is said about this Ball game.

My nice house and garden are important to me although the furthest I have been in the garden since last summer is a trip to the bin. Being confined to the house and also approaching ninety years old is a challenging state of affairs but knowing my garden is at the back door is vital to me and I look forward the warmer days of summer when I can once more enjoy the sun. One tangible salvation is the Lap Top which allows me to spend time writing about my family history. This may be less than compelling to some but I cannot overstate the fact that it has been key to my survival in helping me through looking after George.. Sometimes I wonder if I enjoy dwelling in the past and digging up old memories but so what if I do it gets me through the day and does not really matter. How people lived and survived in the past interests me so perhaps my memories will be enjoyed by some in the future. Some smart medic has discovered recently that if older people are asked a question about their past a part of the brain starts to function and the more they think about it more is remembered. I found this out when I first wrote stories and was amazed at the episodes I could recall when I thought deeply about it.

We have now moved into April and sunnier days emerging from a lonely winter but preparing for summer days which can only be good.

The main purpose of this story was George and myself and our journey through dementia which has been told so I feel now is the time to finish as my life now is very quiet and uneventful as would be expected of someone my age. I manage to function in my own home at a slow pace and may this continue. Story writing was all new to me but it helped me through difficult times and kept me balanced so it served its purpose.

18th September 2015

Here I am again when I thought I had run out of words but an important occasion is approaching on the 15th October when George will have been dead for one year. We have all gone through this sad time in our different ways. As far as I am concerned it has been difficult with some low, some very low periods but also happy memories. Funny we remember all the good times and the not so good are blacked out which is probably a survival device. All I know is that it has been the hardest time of my life and I have had a few. Being alone is the worst part helped by Sheila and Lesley who have always given support. Being one after being two for seventy years takes a lot of getting used to and learning to live with this is heavy going but having no choice we come through.

I have a very comfortable home. No money worries also a nice garden so this is a bonus. To be able to keep this going with help, some paid takes a load off my mind as I am choosing to stay in my home as long as possible and hopefully forever as I am uneasy about Care Homes. Also I have good neighbours and two long term friends who live nearby so this is important. So not time yet to be 'looked after' and just be a number on a door in a corridor.

Being an independent person it is not easy to depend on others but I suppose I am past my sell by date now so have to bow to the inevitable. Sheila and Lesley make it east by taking me shopping and I only have to phone one of them if I run out of any item and it appears.

Sheila Hancock the actress has been rabbiting on about there being no need to be lonely when one partner is left alone. Just join a club and get out in the world says she meeting people. That comes from one who is able to get around and fair enough but does not solve the problems of those whose legs will not allow this. She possibly means well but being an actress hardly gives her the ability to give advice.

My two daughters are entirely different individuals and not alike at all but this is good as it balances matters .It is sometimes hard to believe that they came from the same parents {but they did}. Sheila finds it difficult to 'open up' about her feelings which is a bit like her dad . After all she kept Andrew a secret from us all for many years which floored me. She proved she could keep secrets from her closest friends but sometimes this can be isolating. Lesley on the other hand pours her heart out but that way you get things off your chest which can be good. I suppose we are the way we are made so just have to get on with what we are given. I do worry sometimes about the demands I must put on them as I can remember the four years I looked after my own parents more so when my mum died and dad was left alone and more or less blind. There were times it was tiring but they were both very independent and looked after themselves as best they could and I and Alastair filled in for the things they could not do so I have no regrets. Care Homes were not an option if I remember right so it was either home or hospital. They did not own a vacuum or fridge so this made looking after them more challenging but I still managed walking the dog to visit them usually on a Saturday night and mum walked with me and the dog to the Park on the return journey so we had our moments of normality also..

It would be possible for Sheila and Lesley to get together and share the time they spend with me thus giving them more time to themselves but neither of them would listen to me as they do their own thing. Unlike George I still have my marbles even though mobility lets me down but having a clear mind lets me understand the pressure I put on them whereas George accepted things without regard because of his medical condition. I do my best as far as house cleaning and gardening having the cash to be able to do this. Despite all the labour saving devices around now life seems to be lived at a very high speed trying to reach the impossible. What has happened to 'What is this life if full of care we have no time to stand and stare'? Take a step back and find out what really matters.

.

September 23rd has approached which is Lesley's birthday and our wedding anniversary but as the title of this saga says it is Nancy Alone and so an entirely different anniversary with one half not here. There have been sad moments to-day but I have to be grateful for the many years we did have together. There was a great grandson born today so life goes on.

October has arrived so winter here but the weather has been remarkably good for the time of year. I had a run with Sheila in her car to Killearn this week and the colour of autumn is really stunning in the country. This is a lovely time of year apart from the darkening nights which I do not like.

As I have said before I am not an early riser and to-day Ishbel phoned before I got downstairs so back to sit on bed for half hour blether getting my day eventually started at 11.30am I phoned Mavis next door to tell her that her newspaper had been delivered to my house so we met in my path to hand over her said paper and of course had another blether but Mavis was suddenly overcome by her husband Robert's death which happened a few months ago. She is finding it difficult to come to terms with and I fully understand so there we were hugging in the garden before I even had a cup of tea She was preparing to go to a Lunch Club in her church so this would no doubt sort her out for now. Those feelings Mavis had appear for no reason and have to be dealt with as we do. It was after midday before I finally had a cup of tea and it tasted better than any before. That was a busy morning for me and not the usual boring ones and how a SOON TO BE NOT octogenarian lives.

As I have already said Mavis attends a Lunch Club in her church but this has never been of interest to me. When I was pregnant many moons ago I took the decision to go to a relaxation class for pregnant women. I soon realised it was not for me as the occasional pregnant woman was acceptable but a whole class of them lying on the floor like beached whales trying to relax was too much for me and I never went back. The same applies now to elderly people as a few are fine but not a roomful in various stages of disability. It must be part of the Genes as my dad felt the same when I tried to get him to a Lunch Club near him. He did not think he wqs old enough at eighty to join them. I now understand how he felt.

Now that I am approaching ninety years of age I take stock of my life and weed out the less important parts of my life. I have felt no connection at all to Ben and his family for some time now as although he is my grandson I feel no bond and he has not been in contact with me since George died so he without doubt feels the same. The last thing I want at my time of life is a re – surfacing of the 'Douglas' exhausting times which I know would be difficult to cope with now so I tread warily.

The one big event in my life has come from something I at one time would not have thought possible and it has brought me so much pleasure. I have at last mastered the scooter by becoming Lesley;s trainer. She likes long walks usually about five miles and I tag along with her on the scooter and blether most of the time. We know all the low kerbs in the area and have learned a lot about the scooter including not to try climbing high pavements.

Another important part of the art of scootering is to make sure it has been fully charged as we found out fairly recently when we came to a halt in the park as it was growing dark. Lesley got the car to deposit me home leaving the scooter at the gates of the park, key removed of course. She had then to return to push the scooter uphill. All our nearby relations were not at home that night to help as luck would have it. A tired Lesley appeared plugging scooter in garage to re charge and a lesson learned for the future. I have another story about The Scooter on my lap top so I will not repeat myself here.

27th December 2015
A big event in my uneventful life happened recently as I am now the owner of a Bio Bidet. Andrew fixed the seat to my cloakroom toilet and probably thought I was going mad. I have the cleanest bum in probably Glasgow all thanks to modern technology. At the press of a button my nether regions are washed and the press of another button dries them and also a heated seat which is perfect. Hopefully this will allow me to do my own ablutions should things become more difficult. Enough said about this delicate subject.

5th January 2016
Goodbye to the 'festive season' and welcome 2016 and now to get back to normal living. It remains to be seen how many more aids to surviving ageing will turn up in 2016. I somehow think I have come to the end of the road in gadgets now although there is a very small scooter suitable for going around shops out there somewhere I am more than interested

in but the problem is getting one light enough for my two daughters to get in and out of the car. Still looking……………………….

Part 9. The Broomhill Practice 1934 – 2015

Nancy Barr (nee Chambers) or Annie H Barr as known in the practice recalling memories of the GP Surgery since she first attended as a nine year old in 1934 reminding the family of the great changes in medicine since those early days.
June 2015

Moving to Scotstounhill from Ruchill in1934 we left behind so I'm told a truly lovely caring doctor by the name of Dr Bissett but my only memory of him when visiting for some ailment or other was the fact that he gave my mum and I a run home in his car and I did not get the toffee apple I was promised for obvious reasons. Cars were rare so this was quite an occasion for me. Certainly not likely to happen in the present society with ten minute appointments and the tempo of life to-day but it is called progress.

Dr Bissett put us in touch with Dr Cumming as I think they had trained together thus beginning a long association with a very good medical practice.

When our family appeared on the scene and registered with Dr Cumming the NHS had another fourteen years to materialize. From the little I can remember my dad had insurance through his work. I am unsure how it worked but we seemed to get some free or almost free treatment. The secret then was that we rarely saw a doctor and we were either very healthy or our parents were able to cure most minor ailments.

Dr Cumming consulted at his large house in Victoria Park Drive South and his wife opened the door and showed us into a waiting room and when it was time to see the doctor she showed us into the surgery. She referred to him as 'Doctor'. We were then shown out the front door when consultation finished. A nice civilised society! Maybe worth mentioning here that when the NHS came in to being a letter arrived telling us that unless we were paying patients we had to attend the surgery in Dumbarton Road or Broomhill Drive. I have vague memories of a Surgery in Dumbarton Road but not sure. I must stress that we received the same professional treatment no matter what surgery but we saw ourselves out the door without help when we were non-paying. This perhaps was the start of the do it yourself society leading up to 2015 when touch screen arrived.

Never would I have thought that visiting the Surgery was comparable to climbing Everest. Walking is difficult and I have every walking aid known to man parked in the garage including a Scooter which belonged to George and as the family all know still scares me although I drove a car for fifty years accident free. A car and a scooter are entirely different and I appreciate this. I do persevere but entirely local quiet roads which in those days of cut backs are in a terrible state so this does not help scooter species at all.

It irritates me that my head tells me I can do things but my body cannot. That is the reason for writing those stories from the past and probably boring everyone. It helps keep me sane also I live alone now and have to find something to do. My eyesight is not great so maybe this will be the last one. I doubt typing Guide Dogs have been invented yet.

I have deviated from the Broomhill Practice but this happens occasionally. My last visit to Dr Cumming in his nice house was to see if he had a cure for a bunion. I was eighteen and had very high heels on. He took one look at the shoes and told me if I wore silly shoes like that I would be crippled. He must have been psychic and he was proved correct although I do not really believe my troubles to-day are due to the high heels. When his wife showed me out the door I noticed she had very flat shoes and probably no bunions. No-one would stop me wearing high heel shoes at that time of my life when scarcities during the war were in abundance. Those particular shoes were sent all the way from Egypt by George who was serving in the army at that time so they were rather special.

The year 1941 was not a good year for the family. During the Clydebank blitz our house was almost demolished by a bomb and my dad and I emerged shaken but no serious injuries apart from our dog who never fully recovered. I cannot imagine that there would be many patients attending the Surgery the day after the Blitz as we were all in a state of shock and hardly aware of injuries. A few bombs fell near the Surgery but not much damage done. Lucky to have survived we were now homeless and stayed with friends for many months. I will not repeat myself as I have said all this in 'Nancy's Story' To get back to the .Broomhill Practice the next episode is relevant how the Health Service was in the 1940's.

Soon after the blitz I took ill with an ovarian cyst and was referred to Dr McKay Hart at the Western Infirmary. He was a young up and coming gynaecologist and showed great interest in my case as he thought it unusual in a fourteen year old. His interest was such that for him to be able to perform the operation which was required he arranged I go into a private nursing home in Burnbank Gardens at his expense. I was three weeks in Burnbank Nursing Home half the time spent in bed. It was quite a novelty to me as I had never been ill before and probably enjoyed the attention. I was awakened after the operation by air raid sirens as I lay vulnerable in bed remembering my experiences from a few months back. However a helpful nurse assured me that if bombs fell I would be put under the bed. This did not seem to bother me as I was high on the drugs from the operation and in 1940 it took a long time to come round fully from anaesthetics. Health and safety were way in the future then and I wonder how they would have responded to bombs raining down on a city.

The younger members of my family may be interested to know there may have been another member to our clan as the diagnosis of the cyst was thought to have been an unformed twin because it was made up of hair and bone. It ended in a jar on a shelf in the Western Infirmary for goodness knows how long for future medical students to study. Hopefully I furthered Dr McKay Hart's career and I believe he became a Professor. Ten years later Douglas was born with Dr McKay Hart in attendance but I doubt he remembered much about me as he progressed up the ladder. This time we had to pay for treatment.

My memories of the remainder of the war years and the Surgery are not clear. I know that Dr Calder and Dr Cumming were there. Dr Dickson was a POW in the Far East I think Burma and was badly treated as were all POW's. He luckily came home but was almost unrecognisable but in time he seemed to make a full recovery. My teen years were spent during wartime with warnings from mum that four nights a week Ballroom dancing would ruin my health but this being our favourite pastime I never listened and came through unscathed. TB and other illnesses were prevalent and one of my friends was in hospital a year recovering from TB. Our generation exercised lots and we seemed healthy enough despite wartime food or maybe even because of it

However there were lots of infectious illnesses around at this time and when I first met George his parents and sister were in hospital at the same time with Scarlet Fever. Their house and bedding were fumigated each time one of them took ill. In 1942 there was a Smallpox outbreak and we stood in long queues in central Glasgow at a health clinic for inoculation which gave us a very sore arm. I've been lead away from my story again but thought it worth mentioning.

The Surgery at one time was further down Broomhill Drive and at that time appointments were available in the evening and on Saturday mornings. One of the doctors in the practice was also on duty during the night and this was done by rota. The waiting room had rows of chairs and it was a case of watching your turn in the queue but some patients waited for a particular doctor so this could be confusing and when the voice at the door called 'next please' one or two patients would stand up and all had to be sorted out but usually quite civilised. It was often around two hours spent in the smoke laden surgery with coughs and sneezes we probably went home with more bugs than we came in with.

Antibiotics must have arrived about this time and was the wonder drug of the time. The medicine of my childhood was a spoonful of cod liver oil every day and I loathed it but it must have done something for my bones so maybe worthwhile. Chemical Food was another disgusting medicine which I think contained iron so had to be taken through a straw as it discoloured the teeth. This medicine was usually given to us after the regular childhood illnesses supposedly to help us back to health.

My Gran came to live with us in the mid 1940's as she had dementia and Dr Cumming was supportive but not a lot to be done. No sizeable change in 2015 as still no cure. She eventually ended up in the Southern General Hospital as her illness progressed. We travelled to see her on the Whiteinch Ferry to Govan in all weathers and as it was a small ferry in windy weather it was carried up the Clyde but came to our destination in time. As I am writing this the Southern General is now a top new hospital and greatly enlarged so how about a nice new ferry to ease the transport situation?

Dr Cumming was in attendance when our second child Sheila was born at Homeland Nursing Home in 1955. He was a believer in mother having a rest as long as possible after the birth as there would not be much chance of relaxation for quite some time with a young baby. He also paid extra attention to Douglas who was four years old to avoid him being eclipsed by the new baby. He always had a sweet for him which would be frowned on today in our perfect society. This worked a year or so later when Douglas wet the bed and Dr Cumming instead of prying into his mind to find the reason offered him a sweet if he was dry for a week. He managed this with a few lapses but Douglas enjoyed being the centre of attention so I was never certain which helped the most.

Sadly in 1957 Dr Cumming died suddenly during an Asian flu outbreak which greatly shocked everyone who knew him as he never seemed to be ill. I remember him attending two elderly ladies who lived near us and seeing me in the garden asked me to get a prescription at the chemist for them. Such was his caring school of thought.

It almost seems immoral now that during the 1940's a doctor in the Surgery advised my mum to try smoking for her symptoms of the menopause. Smoking was accepted then and there were large placards lit up at night telling you the benefits of cigarettes. Smoke was everywhere and in theatres and cinemas we watched through a haze of smoke. I was a non-smoker but must have inhaled enough smoke in my day to class myself as ten a day at least. Doctors also had their ash trays on the desk with many stubbed out cigarettes. Oddly enough I do not mind the smell of cigarette smoke and I am sure the reason is that it brings back memories of my younger days. A bit like Evening in Paris perfume which was in abundance during the war years. The younger generation will not remember this particular perfume but it was our only choice in the 1940's.

Lesley was born in 1963 at home with Dr Walker in attendance. Dr Walker came into the practice after Dr Cumming died if my memory serves me right and about the same time Dr Clark replaced Dr Calder so lots of changes. Dr Dickson was the other doctor at this time.

Thalidomide was around when you were born Lesley and I was so pleased when Dr Walker advised me not to take this drug because of sickness as there were thought to be some problems about it. Good advice here as was proved by the deformities in lots of children.

The abnormal effect of some over the counter drugs was the cause of mum's death as she died from cirrhosis of the liver taking Paracetamol self-medicating for Migraine headaches. She was proud of the fact that she rarely saw a doctor as she was usually in good health but in 1973 when she died I doubt if doctors were fully aware of the dangers. Dr Walker was puzzled by her illness as it was often associated with alcoholics ruling her out. Paracetamol was sold in large bottles then and when mum died there were a few found in the house. Hopefully a nasty death like mums would not happen now thanks to the advances of medical science.

Lesley had a severe attack of measles when she was two years old and the treatment was to keep her in a darkened room till her temperature lowered for whatever reason. Happily she had no ill effects and with vaccination now this illness and others have been almost eradicated. Maybe the Health Service is not as it should be in 2015 but we should appreciate the advances that have been made.

It was a surprise when Dr Walker left the Surgery around 1974 for a desk job with the National Health Service. I have the notion that he left because of the pressures of being a GP. I know that when mum died he felt sad that she had not seen him sooner and maybe prevent a needless death but unfortunately she was her own medical woman. Dr Whitty followed him into the Surgery soon after and was a good replacement.

Sister Hussey was in the practice around the 1980's and a very caring nurse with an interest in us as a family. However she was one to be obeyed as I discovered myself when I tried to reduce my weight because of blood pressure. I had a diet of vegetable soup, vegetables, fruit and very little fat if any at all. She told me that I was to get two pounds off each week – no more, no less. If I did not I would be at risk of a stroke so no choice there.

The long and short of it was that I did manage to reduce my weight by two stones which I was pleased about but I did not feel particularly well and later I was diagnosed with depression which I would not wish on anyone. Dr Whitty was very understanding and watched me closely till the Prozac kicked in. Lesley was pregnant with Lucy and off work with a broken ankle. She came every morning, crutches and all, to help me sort out my day. All she needed in her condition was a mother struggling to get through every minute.

Time passed till one day Lesley and I were in town and I had this extreme urge for chips. My appetite had been poor till then. We walked into British Home Stores and had a large bowl of the nicest chips I had ever tasted or so they seemed to me. I never told Sister Hussey as she would have been horrified. That was the end of diets for me as I was convinced that the lack of fats caused this horrible chapter in my life although the medical profession would probably disagree. I settled being aware of the foods I ate and medication to keep my blood pressure ok. The fringe benefit of depression was that my weight came down another stone but not to be recommended. Sister Hussey and I parted at this stage but I think on good terms. Family support was so important in getting me out of this black hole I had tumbled into and I was extremely thankful it was there.

The icing on the cake Lucy is that you were born on my birthday 6th November so what not to be happy about?

Sister Stewart succeeded Sister Hussey in the practice probably about the 1990's. Like her predecessor she shows an interest in her patients and their family being caring and helpful. She is an outdoor person which must help compensate her for the trials of her job.

Medicines have changed so much since 1934 but the Broomhill Practice has always tried to keep up with the times and improving their premises for the benefit of the patient so it was a correct decision for our family to join this professional team.

In my eighty years association with the surgery our family never had any disputes so that must prove something. My one issue was with Dr Clark but nothing serious merely not singing from the same hymn sheet possibly.

Our present team of doctors in 2015 are following in the footsteps of their predecessors keeping up the same standards. Dr Marshall has our special thanks for helping us through very difficult times recently with the death of George after his long struggle with dementia.

I have just about run out of steam about The Broomhill Practice but it seems pertinent to mention that at the present moment Lucy has just qualified as a Pharmacist and we are all proud of her hard work and great great Gran Hunter who gave a lot of her time to the Suffragette movement would have been equally pleased a female ancestor had reached such heights..

Just watch out Lucy your wee sister Kirsty is hot on your heels ....

Printed in Great Britain
by Amazon